Elvis' DNA

Proves

He's Alive

By

Bill Beeny

BRANDEN BOOKS
Boston

Library of Congress Cataloging-in-Publication Data

Beeny, Bill, 1926-.
  Elvis' DNA proves he's alive / by Bill Beeny. –1st ed.
    p.cm.
Includes bibliographical references (p.   ) and index.
  ISBN 0-8283-2089-6 (pbk. : alk. paper))
  1. Presley, Elvis, 1935-1977– Death and burial.
  2. Rock musicians – United States – Biography. I. Title.

ML420.P96B45 2005
782.42166'092 – dc22

                                                    2004026830

BRANDEN BOOKS
Division of Branden Publishing Company, Inc.
P.O. Box 812094
Wellesley MA 02482

CONTENTS

DEDICATION

Elvis Aron Presley, wherever you may be. Your music and your life have brought joy to millions. At our "Everything's Elvis" store at the Union Station Mall, hundreds of people pass daily and look at our TV monitor with your singing. It always puts a smile on their faces. This week I received a call from a lady in Australia. She said because her child was autistic she had been bitter. Then someone sent her an album of your songs. She said, "It changed my whole life, especially the gospel songs." Thank you Elvis, for being you.

THANK YOU

I want to just ramble here, and say thank you to the hundreds of people who have made my research and this book possible.

A very special thanks to my unnamed doctor friend in Memphis, and my attorney son, Andrew Beeny–without both of you, the DNA discovery would not have been possible. Thousands of other Elvis fans and I are indebted to you for making the truth known concerning the DNA of Elvis.

Thanks to my friend, *Buffalo* Jody Owen for his contribution. To my long time secretary, Dolores, for her untiring work, and my son, Pete, for his computer help. Thanks to my son, Toby, for doing the editing, and preparing the manuscript for the publishers.

Thanks to our Elvis researchers, Phil Aitcheson and Gail Brewer-Giorgio, America's leading Elvis is Alive exponents. Their research has been invaluable to me.

Then a special thanks to all my friends in the media who have come to the museum to film, write, and air the truth about Elvis being alive. They include my friends from ABC, CBS, NBC, the film crew from CNN in Atlanta, as well as those from "A Current Affair," the After Breakfast crew, The Family Channel, Adair Kaiser, producer from the world's largest cable network, Encore-Brendon Conway, producer at CNBC in New York for inviting me up, John Pertzborn from NBC, Paul Shankman, ABC, and our radio personalities in Germany, Ireland, Holland, Sweden and Norway.

Thanks to those in Australia and the film crew from *Globo*, Brazil's national television network. They flew all the way from Rio De Janeiro, Brazil to film us.

A very, very special thanks to the Wake-Up Crew in Memphis, Tennessee, on Rock 102, Memphis's most listened to station. Boys, without you, none of this would have been possible. Thanks! In a very special way, you are super!

Thanks to Paul Harvey of ABC for his coverage, and CBN, the Canadian Broadcast Network that covers all of Canada, and the Public Broadcast network with its hundreds of stations.

Last, but not least, I want to thank Rosie O'Donnell for her invitation to be on her show! Even though she cancelled me while I was flying up to New York, she replaced my spot on the show with jumping frogs. The frogs and I thank you, Rosie, for without you giving these frogs their start in television, they would never have made it to stardom in the Budweiser ads!

Bill Beeny

INTRODUCTION:
Why Write This Book?

Elvis Presley has perhaps been written about more than any other person in the last twenty years. Some wrote to praise him, others to vilify. Some wrote insisting that he was indeed dead. How he died, they could not agree. There are eight different views by the experts as to how he died. Some concluded variously that it was drugs, suicide, murder, compacted colon, heart attack, bone cancer, or that he choked on his own vomit. So, say the experts. The definition of an expert is that X is an unknown quantity and a *spert* is a drip under pressure.

There have been many books written contending that none of the above is true. The reason experts can't agree on the cause of Elvis' "death" is because he is not dead! Several books and booklets have been written on this subject. In these *Elvis Is Alive* books, much helpful information has been documented. Several authors have labored months digging out facts that prove to any open-minded person that indeed, Elvis Presley did, for a very valid reason, fake his death.

Many national surveys on the subject have revealed that a large percentage of the population in the U.S. believe that Elvis Presley is alive today. "A Current Affair" sent a crew from New York to film our Elvis Is Alive Museum in Wright City,

Missouri. They filmed for eight hours, asking me questions as to why I believed Elvis is alive. They showed this film six times. On one show, they conducted a national poll, asking the viewers to call in and say whether they felt Elvis was alive or dead. The response was overwhelming. Their phones were tied up for days.

The conclusion was that 54% thought he was dead while a whopping 46% said he was alive. So, nearly half the people in this survey concluded that the King of Rock and Roll is alive today, some twenty years after his supposed death. That's incredible! It also puts at rest the idea that any who believe that Elvis faked his death are part of a fringe group. But why write another book on the subject? Because one thing could settle this controversy–a DNA test!

CHAPTER ONE

For the past six years I have read everything concerning Elvis that I could get my hands on. I read the good, the bad, the trashy and the tantalizing. I have traveled thousands of miles across this country interviewing people and searching for evidence. During this time, I have been interviewed by major television network editors, and by talk shows, newspapers, and magazines editors from around the world.

Because of these interviews, people have contacted me with very valuable information on the subject of Elvis being alive. This information has been priceless.

I was invited to fly to New York to appear on the Rosie O'Donnell Show, and to go on the *Late Nite* at CNBC to deate Elvis' bodyguards on the subject of Elvis being alive. I have sat in the home of a prominent doctor and read a copy of the full autopsy report produced at the Baptist Memorial Hospital in Memphis. The original copy of this autopsy report was sealed by court order, not to be opened until 2025. Geraldo Rivera and ABC sued to get a copy of this autopsy report, and were turned down by the court. And here I was, holding in my hands, and reading, the full autopsy report that they could not get!

It was then that I discovered that tissue samples from a liver biopsy, and also, the tissue done by what was reputed to be Elvis' corpse, were also available. Here, at last, was the final proof as to whether Elvis was alive or not! So, this is the reason for this book. For the first time in history, we were able to test Elvis' living tissue with that of the corpse in the casket. And this, as you will read, is exactly what we did.

Of all of the hundreds of interviews I have given in the last few years, there was one, which stood out above the others. It was with Rock 102 radio, the "Wake-Up Crew" in Memphis. This is perhaps the most listened to radio show in the area.

I have been on the show many times by phone, and also in person. They are the most courteous hosts you could ever have. It was from these interviews that I developed some of my most valuable documented information about Elvis being alive. (It was here that we obtained a copy of the footprint of the real Lisa Marie Presley, thus proving that Michael Jackson's former wife is a stand-in and not the real Lisa Marie. But that is another story for another time.)

The Wake-Up Crew also interviewed my son, Andrew Beeny, on Rock 102. After the telephone interview, he received a phone call from a prominent Memphis doctor who was interested in the subject that my son was discussing on the air. The doctor invited Andrew and me to his home in Memphis, where he said he could show us a lot of information about Elvis. We took him up on his offer.

My son has his own law firm in St. Louis, but he arranged his schedule so that he and I could drive to Memphis and meet with the doctor. In this book, I will not use the doctor's name. He is a prominent Memphis physician and has his own clinic. He is also the physician for some important people who were closely associated with Elvis. If his name were used the powers that be at Graceland could put a great deal of pressure on him as well as some of his peers. He is also a very busy doctor and does not want to get caught up in the media merry-go-round, and get distracted from his profession. So, I am honoring my promise to him to not reveal his identity in this book or any of my media interviews. I am very much indebted to him for the valuable information he has given me.

We drove to the doctor's home, which turned out to be more of a mansion. Its size would compare to Graceland, iron gates and all. He and his family showed us real southern hospitality. As we sat in the living room, the doctor left and returned with a large stack of papers. He told me that here was a copy of Elvis' paperwork. Here, in print, were all of the reports from every day that Elvis stayed in the Baptist Memorial Hospital. He checked in under name Aaron Sivle, which, of course, is Elvis spelled backwards. Elvis often used this alias to avoid people knowing who he was.

Also, in the volume of papers that the doctor gave me to read was the *full autopsy report* on the body. It seems that the doctor who befriended us had also been a friend of Dr. Harold Sexton, one of the pathologists who had helped perform the autopsy on Elvis. Dr. Sexton was fearful of all the controversy that swirled around the death of Elvis. Wild rumors were flying! There were charges and counter charges. The cries of "cover up" dominated headlines. There were threats of lawsuits. Some might involve the doctors and pathologists who participated in the autopsy. So, Dr. Sexton did the only logical thing he could do. He made copies of everything they did, to protect himself in the event he was sued.

Immediately after Elvis' so-called death, the family ordered an autopsy performed on the body, on the advice of their lawyers. By doing this, the family could seal the autopsy from the public. If the Medical Examiner ordered the autopsy then it would have been open to the public. The court sealed this autopsy until 2025.

Dr. Sexton, however, made a full copy of the autopsy report in order to protect himself. Here I was reading the famed, sealed autopsy report which the *Rivera Live* and ABC could not get by a lawsuit!

In the full autopsy report the body was weighed in at 170 lbs, which is also the weight recorded on the medical examiner's report. Well, it is a known fact that at this time in his career, Elvis was extremely heavy, in fact over 250 lbs. So, this

170 lb. body could not possibly have been Elvis Presley. Here it was, in black and white, in the full autopsy report.

Also, in the report there was mention of a long scar, running perpendicular on the chest. The scar had been healed for some time. An old chest operation was evident on the cadaver, which the autopsy was performed on... but Elvis had never had such an operation. So again, this cadaver could not possibly be Elvis. There were also numerous other inconsistencies revealed in the full autopsy report.

During our lengthy and interesting visit with the doctor, it was also determined that he not only had Elvis' lifelong Baptist Hospital records, but also the autopsy report, and actual <u>body tissue of Elvis!</u>

Elvis had two biopsy tests. Both of the biopsy specimens came from his liver. He had one biopsy on 10/15/73 and the other on 1/28/75. These biopsy samples of liver tissue were taken to determine if he had hepatitis or not. His mother, Gladys Presley, had died of hepatitis complications. It was determined that Elvis did not have Hepatitis. But, here were several body tissue samples of Elvis. Here are photocopies of the reports of Elvis being in the hospital for these biopsies.

As you can see from the following Baptist Memorial Hospital reports, Elvis had two biopsies: one in 1973, the other in 1975. In 1973, he checked in the hospital under the alias of Aaron Sivle. He was in room 1502 and his doctor was L.D. Wrumble. On 10/29/73, the doctor's report showed "Mild fatty change, focal liver cell necrosis, and occasional PAS positive Kupffer cells suggesting toxic effect," but no hepatitis. Dr. Robert I. Lerman, M.D, signed this report.

Then, on 2/11/75, Elvis checked back into the Baptist Memorial Hospital with apparently the same problem he had two years previously. This time he again checked in under the alias Aaron Sivle, but with his father's address, 1293 Old Hickory. Again, he submitted to a biopsy. Again, they took a liver specimen. These were very small specimens.

On 2/14/75, Dr. George C. Bales issued a lengthy report (which we have reproduced here), which basically was about the same as the first report. No life-threatening disease, no hepatitis. There was again fatty liver tissue and some toxicity.

So, having confirmed that we had two liver specimens which the hospital records confirmed were indeed tissue samples of the biopsy of Elvis, we needed something with which to compare them. Note: the numbers on the slides of tissues match the numbers on the hospital records.

There were numerous and large specimens from the autopsy of the body which was reputed to be that of Elvis. Here again, we photograph a page of the autopsy report and again, these tissue numbers match the ones sent to the laboratory.

With tissue from the biopsy (living Elvis) and with tissue from the autopsy (dead "Elvis") we were ready for them to be sent to the laboratory that studies DNA. If they matched then Elvis was dead. If they did not match, then Elvis was alive. If the body in the casket was not Elvis, it was a donor body. But whose body was in the casket? Was the grave at Graceland about to cry out the truth? The DNA held the answer to these and other questions.

My attorney son had often used laboratories in paternal cases that dealt with blood tests and with the accurate science of DNA marking. He selected LAB CORP of Burlington, North Carolina to have the specimens sent for analysis. The specimens were sent under the names of John Doe so that no one knew that they were actually testing the samples of Elvis' body tissue. To make it look like a paternity case, we also sent the DNA sample of a young woman, as though we wanted to know who her father was. We wanted a fair and accurate analysis of Elvis' two tissues, if in fact they were both from Elvis. The last thing we wanted was his fame to influence the outcome of the test.

Even though I felt certain that Elvis faked his death, and that he was alive today, I wanted a fair and impartial DNA test. I told both the doctor and my son that if the DNA test proved

Elvis was dead I would accept it. I knew we had the right body samples. I told them that if the DNA laboratory tissues matched, then Elvis was dead, and I would close the doors to the Elvis is Alive Museum. Also, I would call a news conference and apologize for promoting something that was not true. I had no desire whatsoever in promoting an agenda that was false.

Andrew called the laboratory to have them send the specimen containers to the doctor in Memphis so he could mail in the specimens. The laboratory's requirements are particularly rigorous. The doctor must seal the specimens in the containers and sign an affidavit. The courier must sign an affidavit. The technician receiving them must sign an affidavit that says that the containers remained sealed and were not tampered with.

The specimens were sent to the laboratory on 10/23/96. Then the wait began. Was Elvis alive or dead? Would I be closing the museum? A thousand questions raced through my mind.

Finally, on 2/20/97, we got the report back. It was mailed to my son at his law office. He called me late at night to give me the results. He said, "Dad, the DNA report is back. I have bad news and good news for you."

"What is the bad news?"

"The tissue from the 1973 biopsy was not clear enough to get the DNA markings from."

When he said this, my heart sank!

"What about the 1975 biopsy specimens?" I asked.

"It was a good sample with ample markings. Also the autopsy sample was large with a lot of DNA markings."

"Don't keep me in suspense," I exclaimed. "Do the two specimens match?"

"No, they do not. Elvis is alive!"

The living Elvis tissue did not match the tissue from the autopsy! The casket had a donor body; it was not Elvis.

Bill Beeny in front of the Museum

Elvis rode to concerts in the limo that is displayed at the Museum

Hundreds of Elvis pictures in the original museum building

Bill Beeny cutting tape of Elvis songs

BAPTIST MEMORIAL HOSPITAL
899 MADISON AVE. • MEMPHIS, TENNESSEE 38146

SURGICAL PATHOLOGICAL REPORT
E. ERIC MUIRHEAD, M. D., Director

PATH. NO. S73-22029
DATE OF SPECIMEN 10-24-73
DATE OF REPORT 10-24-73

PATIENT NAME: Aaron Sivle
3764 Elvis Presley Blvd., City   AGE: 38 SEX: M   FIRST NAME OF SPOUSE:
ROOM NUMBER: 1502   HOSPITAL NUMBER: 054705
PHYSICIAN: Dr. L.D. Wruble
TISSUE REMOVED: liver biopsy

CLINICAL HISTORY AND DIAGNOSIS: persistent abnormalities

PREVIOUS ACCESSION NUMBERS (SURGICAL PATHOLOGY)

NUMBER OF SLIDES:

GROSS DESCRIPTION:

Received in formalin unlabeled are several small portions of light
brown, soft tissue, the largest of which is 2.5 cm. in length and
0.1 cm. in diameter. The entire specimen will be submitted for
biopsy.

CF:jas

Microscopic Diagnosis: Mild fatty change, focal liver cell
                                  necrosis, and occasional PAS positive
                                  Kupffer cells suggesting toxic effect

                                  10-29-73

jas   Robert I. Lerman, M.D.

Exhibit A

SURGICAL PATHOLOGICAL REPORT

Copy of actual document

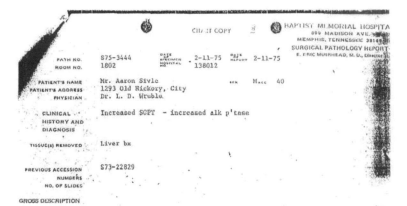

BAPTIST MEMORIAL HOSPITA
899 MADISON AVE.
MEMPHIS, TENNESSEE 38149
SURGICAL PATHOLOGY REPORT
E. ERIC MUIRHEAD, M. D., Director

PATH NO. S75-3444
ROOM NO. 1802

DATE OF SPECIMEN HOSPITAL 2-11-75   DATE OF REPORT 2-11-75
138012

PATIENT'S NAME   Mr. Aaron Sivle
PATIENT'S ADDRESS   1293 Old Hickory, City   SEX M   AGE 40
PHYSICIAN   Dr. L. D. Wruble

CLINICAL HISTORY AND DIAGNOSIS   Increased SGPT - increased alk p'tase

TISSUE(S) REMOVED   Liver bx

PREVIOUS ACCESSION NUMBERS   S73-22829
NO. OF SLIDES

GROSS DESCRIPTION

The specimen is received in formalin and consists of 3 cm. in length of brownish-tan tissue which appears to be needle biopsy of the liver. The entire specimen is submitted for sectioning unlabeled.

JS:rc

MICROSCOPIC DESCRIPTION: Section through this liver biopsy reveals the lobular pattern to be considerably obscured by marked amounts of fatty change. Hepatocytes reveal both large and small vacuole fatty change, which goes on to the fatty cyst of Hartroft. The nuclei reveal poly- puidy grade II-III. There is some condensation of the cytoplasmic organelles in some areas. There is an occasional acidophilic body. There are a few eosinophils in the sinusoids. There is some nodule in lobule formation and some minimal arachnoid type of fibrosis about the portal canals. The Kupffer cells are hyperplastic and contain both a PAS positive diastase resistant material, partial acid fast ma- terial and numerous vacuoles. The portal canals reveal the bile ducts, arteries and veins to be intact, and not particularly unusual. Some of the portal canals are enlarged by an increased amount of fibrous tissue and some of this fibrous tissue extends in the arachnoid fashion out into the adjacent hepatic parenchyma. A few of the portal canals are infiltrated with lymphocytes. Many of them contain macrophages with a content similar to that seen in the Kupffer cells.

The specimen previously seen on this patient on October 24, 1973, our S73-22829, reveals much less fatty change with some small and large vacuoles, but no definite fatty cyst of Hartroft. The lobular pattern generally at that time was apparent and intact. There was a great deal of lipochrome pigment at that time and there still was in the present biopsy. The hepatocytes reveal polypoidy grade II and there was some condensation in the cytoplasm. There were rare eosinophils in the sinusoids and an occasional area where there was hepatocytolysis with a mononuclear cell infiltrate. A rare acidophilic body was also noted. The Kupffer cells were activated and filled with a PAS positive diastase resistant material and partial acid fast material and numerous vacuoles.

The portal canals revealed the veins, arteries and bile ducts to be intact,

Exhibit C
1/2

Copy of actual document

D/c   2-14-75   CH. 21 COPY   BAPTIST MEMORIAL HOSPIT
                                            899 MADISON AVE.
                                            MEMPHIS, TENNESSEE 38146
                                            SURGICAL PATHOLOGY REPORT
                                            E. ERIC MUIRHEAD, M. D., Director

PATH NO.   S75-3444   DATE SPECIMEN 2-11-75   DATE REPORT 2-11-75
ROOM NO.   1802   HOSPITAL NO. 138012

PATIENT'S NAME   Mr. Aaron Sivle   SEX M AGE 40
PATIENT'S ADDRESS   1293 Old Hickory, City
PHYSICIAN   Dr. L. D. Wruble

CLINICAL   Increased SGPT - increased alk p'tase
HISTORY AND
DIAGNOSIS

TISSUE(S) REMOVED   Liver bx

PREVIOUS ACCESSION S73-22029
NUMBERS
NO. OF SLIDES 9

GROSS DESCRIPTION

                              PART II

and not particularly unusual. Macrophages were present in the portal
canals and have a content similar to that in the Kupffer cells. Occasional
eosinophils were seen in the portal canals.

COMMENT: Morphologic changes in this liver are those that one usually
sees with a nutritional lesion of the liver. The rare acidophilic bodies
and eosinophils suggest the possibility of a toxic hepatitic process
in addition to this nutritional alteration. The slight, but definite,
arachnoid fibrosis also speaks to a nutritional origin of the hepato-
cytic lipid contents. The presence of vacuoles within the Kupffer cells
and macrophages is somewhat unusual in this observers experience, but
with the partially acid fast material that they contain and the PAS
positive diastase resistant material, it is suspected that they are
the residua of disintegrating hepatocytes which contained lipid vacuoles
at the time of their demise.

Microscopic Diagnosis: Material compatible with fatty liver
                       (T5600; M5521 28-4)
                       Tissue changes in liver compatible with injury
                       from toxic substance (T5600; E5000 28-4)

                       2-14-75   (28-4)

jas   George F. Bale, M.D.

Exhibit C
2/2

Copy of actual document

BAPTIST MEMORIAL HOSPITAL   12
MEMPHIS, TENNESSEE

DEPARTMENT OF PATHOLOGY
POSTMORTEM PROTOCOL

Name_____ Mr. Elvis Aron Presley _____ Postmortem No._____ A77-160

Age__42___ Sex___Male___ . Hospital No._____ D.O.A.

Admission: Date_____ Hour_____ Attending Physician_George Nichopoulos, M.

Death: Date____8/16/77___ Hour_____ Postmortem: Date__8/16/77____ Hour____

Prosector___Thomas McC. Chesney, M.D._____ Pathologist _____

Code	Final Pathological Diagnoses	Pho
	1. Cardiomegaly with left ventricular hypertrophy	
	2. Coronary atherosclerosis, mild to moderate	
	3. Pulmonary edema, mild to moderate	
	4. Pulmonary aspiration, mild	
	5. Hepatomegaly due only to fatty metamorphosis of liver	
	6. Splenomegaly, mild, mainly congestive	
	7. Arteriolosclerosis of kidneys, moderate	
	8. Nephrosclerosis, mild	
	9. Papillary necrosis, ancient, single papilla, left	
	10. Atherosclerosis of aorta and cerebral arteries, mild	
	11. Livor mortis, pronounced, upper half of body	
	12. Capillary congestion and petechiae, skin, upper half of body	
	13. Chemosis, bilateral, moderate	
	14. Cardiac puncture wounds, recent	
	15. Gastric hemorrhage, recent, mild	
	16. "Soldier's patch", pericardium	
	17. Scar, left inferior eyelid	
	18. Scar, dorsum, right hand	
	19. Scar, left buttock	
	20. Clinical: α₁ antitrypsin deficiency (genotype MS)	

Copy of actual document

Admit no.   175451   8/21/75   Aaron Sivle

Admit no.   054705   10/15/73   Aaron Sivle
       liver biopsy path no.   S73-22829 date 10/24/73

Admit no.   175451   1/28/75   Aaron Sivle
       hematology study 75-H-535   2-5-75
       liver biopsy   S75-3444 date 2-11-75

Autopsy specimens   A77-160

Cytology
Peggy 227-4572

Exhibit B

Copy of actual document

Admit no.   175451   8/21/75   Aaron Sivle

Admit no.   054705   10/15/73   Aaron Sivle
    liver biopsy   path no.   S73-2829 date 10/24/73

Admit no.   175451   1/28/75   Aaron Sivle
    hematology study   75-H-535   2-5-75
    liver biopsy   S75-3444 date 2-11-75

Autopsy specimens   A77-160

Cytology
Peggy 2277572

Exhibit B

Copy of actual document

LabCorp
Laboratory Corporation of America
P.O. Box 2230 Burlington, NC 27216-2230

Page 1 of 1

Account Information

Acct #:   24414345
ATTY R. ANDREW BEENY AND ASSOC
Acct Ref 1:
Acct Ref 2:
Acct Ref 3:
CLAYTO:4, MO 63105

LabCorp Case # C97-010179

Relationship	Party	Race	Date(s) Drawn
Child	DOE, JANE	6B4-5001-0	10/23/1996
Alleged Father	DOE #2, JOHN	71U-5002-0 Caucasian	01/27/1997

DNA Analysis

	HBGG (11p15.5)	HLADQA 1,2 (6p21.3)	D7S8 (7q22-q32)	GYPA (4q31)	GC (4q12-q13)
C	A, B	3, 4	A	B	A, B
AF	A, B	2	B	A	C
PI					

(*This report is on the 1975 biopsy and does not match the autopsy*)
authors note

Conclusion:

The alleged father, JOHN DOE #2, is excluded from paternity in the following systems: D7S8-(7q22-q32), GC- (4q12-q13), HLADQA- 1,2 (6p21.3), GYPA- (4q31). Therefore, he cannot be the biological father of the child, JANE DOE.

Combined Paternity Index: 0 to 1   Probability of Paternity: 0.00%
                                                (for Probability = 0.5)

Uwe Heine, Ph.D.

"OFFICIAL SEAL"
Notary Public, North Carolina
County of Alamance
Pamela Darin
My Commission Expires 4/3/2000

Sworn to and Subscribed before me

2·20·97   at Burlington, N.C.

Copy of actual document

LabCorp
Laboratory Corporation of America
P.O. Box 2230 Burlington, NC 27216-2230

Page 1 of 1

Account Information

Acct #:   24414346
ATTY R. ANDREW BEENY AND ASSOC
Acct Ref 1:
Acct Ref 2:
Acct Ref 3:
CLAYTON, MO 63105

LabCorp Case # C96-065359

Relationship	Party		Race	Date(s) Drawn
Child	DOE, JANE	5B4-5001-0		10/23/1996
Alleged Father	DOE #2, JOHN	6AF-5005-0	Caucasian	10/12/1996

DNA Analysis

	HBGG (11p15.5)	LDLR (19p13.2-13.1)	D7S8 (7q22-q52)	GYPA (4q31)	GC (4q12-q13)	VWF 1,2 (12p13.5-p13.2)
C	A, B	NTYP	A	B	A, B	18
AF	A, B	NTYP	A	NTYP	B, C	14, 19
PI						

DNA Analysis

	CYP19 1,2 (15q21)	F13B 1,2 (1q31-q32.1)	TPOX 1,2 (2p13)
C	1, 2	10, 11	8
AF	2, 3	8, 9	8, 9
PI			

(autopsy specimen)
(author's note)

Conclusion:

The alleged father, JOHN DOE #2, is excluded from paternity in the following systems: F13B- 1,2 (1q31-q32.1), VWF- 1,2 (12p13.3-p13.2), LDLR- (19p13.2-13.1), GYPA- (4q31). Therefore, he cannot be the biological father of the child, JANE DOE.

Combined Paternity Index: 0 to 1

Probability of Paternity: 0.00%
(Prior Probability = 0.5)

Uwe Herle, Ph.D.

OFFICIAL SEAL
Notary Public, North Carolina
County of Alamance
Pamela Dann
My Commission Expires 4/3/2000

Pamela Dann

Sworn to and Subscribed before
2·20·97 at Burlington, N.C.

Copy of actual document

Lois Smith, Elvis' only living aunt is pictured here with Bill Beeny. She contends that Elvis is alive!

People come from around the world because of the interest in Elvis. There is no charge to go through the museum.

Bill Beeny and family

Elvis impersonators with Bill Beeny in front of Museum

CHAPTER TWO

I cannot put into words the feeling of exhilaration I experienced upon hearing the DNA results. After months and years of being called a nut, a lunatic, and a fraud, now my findings were confirmed by the most accurate science in the world.

The following pages are photocopies from the LAB CORP reports. The first is of the bad specimens, which were not large enough. The next is of the 1975 living Elvis biopsy. The next is of the body they did the autopsy on. You will note that the markings on the last two do not match. The other markings on all the pages identified with a C, is that of the young lady to whom went specimens to make it look as though it were a paternity case. The initials A.F. stand for alleged father.

While this is a very exacting and highly technical science, these final reports are very clear. They "shout to the heavens" that the living Elvis tissue does not match the autopsy tissue. Look at the LAB CORP reports again. The markings are different.

Elvis had been able to pull off the hoax of the century, and for a good reason. Most likely, he did it with the help of the FBI. We will get into that later on. I want to make it clear that in faking his death, he broke no laws. No life insurance money was collected, even though he had a multi-million dollar policy with Lloyds of London. None of the family ever collected a penny on that policy. If they had, that would have been felony fraud. Elvis cashed in two paid-up policies before the funeral for something over one million dollars. That money was legally his. It disappeared when he went into hiding.

Why would Elvis fake his death?

That question is asked of me more than any other. Why would a man of great fame, wealth, and power want to disappear from the public and fake his death? There are many reasons why it was urgent that Elvis fake his death. Time and space do not permit me to elaborate on all of them, but I will touch on the main reasons.

1. Elvis was heavily involved in helping the FBI and the DEA.

Many people are surprised to learn that Elvis requested of President Nixon that he be appointed as a Federal DEA agent at large. (See Elvis' letter written to President Nixon while on a plane en route to Washington D.C.) This exhibit follows. President Nixon appointed Elvis to this position. Many say it was only an honorary title. This is not true.

Elvis was not only given a badge, he was also given a "Black Book" that listed all the DEA agents and undercover agents as well. This would never have been given out with an "honorary" badge. Elvis also had an undercover agent play in his band while doing undercover work for the government. (See our exhibit where the Justice Department sent Elvis a letter thanking him for providing cover for this agent from 1974 through 1976.) Here we see Elvis participating in a three-year federal investigation.

But Elvis' most dangerous mission was in assisting the FBI in "Operation Fountain Pen." This was the largest FBI investigation of the 70's. It was worldwide, involving hundreds of agents. The investigation centered on a Mafia group called The Fraternity. It was a con group that was swindling banks and individuals out of billions of dollars a year. It was directed by a criminal named Peter Frederick Pro.

The FBI used Elvis and a Jet Star plane he was selling for a sting operation against the mob. The sting worked and the mob leaders were arrested. Elvis was to be the chief witness against them. It was then that death threats began to pour in. The last year Elvis performed, he received over three hundred death threats. Something had to be done to protect him. One of the arrested mob members turned on his pals and became a federal witness. He was immediately put into a Federal Witness Protection Program.

If it was dangerous for this mobster, then how much more dangerous was it for Elvis? In fact, Elvis was supposed to testify before a Federal Grand Jury in Memphis the very day of his supposed funeral. This undercover work for the Feds made it imperative that Elvis fake his death to protect himself and his family.

2. Elvis had nagging health problems.

While Elvis' involvement with the DEA and the FBI was his primary reason for faking his death, his health was also a factor. Elvis was under tremendous pressure, which affected his health. He was being treated for glaucoma, which affected his vision. He wore glasses and sunglasses. His eyes were sensitive to extreme light. He was treated for a twisted colon and had to use medication to endure the pain. There was pressure from the tremendous demand for his time. The last year he performed, he did 153 concerts, most of these in different cities. This, in itself, was a grueling schedule.

Elvis also had an antitrypsin deficiency (genotype MS) condition. This, like the AIDS virus, attacks the immune system. He was highly susceptible to colds, flu, and bronchial conditions that consequently had him in and out of the hospital.

Then, there were the liver problems. As mentioned earlier, he had two biopsy tests for hepatitis–one of these in 1973, and the other in 1975. While these tests were negative, it was discovered that there were fatty traces in the liver and some toxicity.

Now it is evident that none of these medical problems was life threatening. Nevertheless, he was in pain. He was under pressure beyond description and these conditions were going to get worse, not better. So, this was another reason why Elvis needed a way out. After the funeral, in an interview, Elvis' manger Colonel Parker remarked that "Elvis needed a way out and I showed him one."

3. Financial Problems

Many people are surprised to learn that at the time of his funeral, Elvis had huge financial problems. He had to push himself daily to do concerts just to pay the bills for that day. Elvis made and spent millions of dollars. He was, without a doubt, the highest paid entertainer. While he was making one million dollars, movie stars like Marilyn Monroe and Elizabeth Taylor were making less than one hundred thousand dollars a movie.

Money had little meaning to Elvis once he had made enough for himself and his family. Both he and his father, Vernon Presley, were poor businessmen. Vernon received $75,000 a year being his business manager. Vernon, with just a grade school education, was sincere and honest with Elvis' money management, but this was not enough.

Colonel Parker took advantage of this and skimmed off a 50% fee as manager of Elvis. This was unheard of. Later, after the funeral, the District Court reprimanded him for this, and stopped all his financial dealings with Elvis Presley Enterprises.

Then there was the heavy expense of running Graceland. Elvis had a large entourage of bodyguards, musicians, backup singers, stage men, sound and lighting people, pilots for his three jets, groundskeepers and so on goes the list. Just maintaining Graceland required several thousands of dollars a day. He had to have relief from this tremendous financial burden and all the daily upkeep. On top of this, since Elvis never took any deductions on his taxes, the IRS took over one half of his income. I am sure it must have seemed to him that financially he was carrying the world on his back.

Elvis was extremely generous. He gave millions to charities, distant relatives, workers, strangers, and any who were in need. He always felt he could make more money. Having been raised dirt poor, and seeing his parents unable to pay their bills, he was always ready to help others in those conditions. Thus, he had to get away from this terrible financial burden.

4. Problems with the Memphis Mafia

Elvis had a mix-match of people he employed, who were constantly around him at Graceland. This was his social life since it was not possible for him to socialize in public because of his fame.

They were named the "Memphis Mafia" because Elvis had them wear black suits and dark sunglasses. Their appearance was like those in the real Mafia. So he started calling them the Memphis Mafia. Some of these were sincere and hard working, and loved Elvis. Some were his relatives. He employed a lot of his relatives. Others were hangers-on who used Elvis. Their only concern was to get what they could get out of him.

There was always bickering between members of the Memphis Mafia. They were jealous of one another in their relationships with Elvis. If he gave one a car, the rest would resent it because they did not get one. Once Elvis determined he was going to fake his death and get out of the pressure cooker he had been in, he began to fire certain members of his group. He terminated the services of Marty Lacker, Red West, Sonny West, and several others. Many of these terminated ex-aides began to publish books that vilified Elvis. The fact that he had taken them when they had nothing and gave them a good living and friendship meant nothing to them. Their attitude was, if the goose can't keep giving me the golden eggs, then let's kill the goose.

Elvis again had to have relief from this bickering and back-stabbing. It broke his heart when Sonny and Red West along with Dave Hebbler, wrote a book vilifying him. He had to have a way out, and he took it by faking his own death.

The second most asked question I have received was, "If Elvis wasn't in the casket, then whose body was it?" This has been a question I have researched for the past six years. Many hold the view that it was a wax dummy. It did not look like Elvis. It looked much younger. Some have speculated there was an air conditioner in the casket because of the weight. They casket weighed around nine hundred pounds. Some reported, "sweat" on the corpse's brow. Dead people don't sweat. What was the answer?

Little by little, the truth began to come out. In the book "Elvis Aaron Presley" by Alanna Nash, she quoted Elvis' cousin, Billy Smith, and Marty Lacker who were both close associates of Elvis. Elvis ex-aides recalled how Elvis told them that he was sick of the life he was living and wanted out. He stated that he had met a terminally ill man who asked for his help. An arrangement was made for the man to donate his body upon death. His body would be put in Graceland and Elvis would disappear. The aides said Elvis had the man make several trips to a plastic surgeon to have some facial features changed to make him look more like Elvis. In return, Elvis promised the terminally ill man he would financially take care of the man's family as long as he lived. The deal was agreed upon. Billy Smith said he didn't believe Elvis' story. However, he later said that the man called him and confirmed it.

Nixon Replies To Elvis

THE WHITE HOUSE
WASHINGTON
December 21, 1970

MEMORANDUM

THE WHITE HOUSE
WASHINGTON

December 21, 1970

MEMORANDUM FOR: MR. H. R. HALDEMAN

FROM: DWIGHT L. CHAPIN

SUBJECT: Elvis Presley

Attached you will find a letter to the President from Elvis Presley. As you are aware, Presley showed up here this morning and has requested an appointment with the President. He states that he knows the President is very busy, but he would just like to say hello and present the President with a gift.

As you are well aware, Presley was voted one of the ten outstanding young men for next year and this was based upon his work in the field of drugs. The thrust of Presley's letter is that he wants to become a "Federal agent at large" to work against the drug problem by communicating with people of all ages. He says that he is not a member of the establishment and that drug culture types, the hippie elements, the SDS, and the Black Panthers are people with whom he can communicate since he is not part of the establishment.

I suggest that we do the following:

This morning Bud Krogh will have Mr. Presley in and talk to him about drugs and about what Presley can do. Bud will also check to see if there is some kind of an honorary agent at large or credential of some sort that we can provide for Presley. After Bud has met with Presley, it is recommended that we have Bud bring Presley in during the Open Hour to meet briefly with the President. You know that several people have mentioned over the past few months that Presley is very pro the President. He wants to keep everything private and I think we should honor his request.

I have talked to Bud Krogh about this whole matter, and we both think that it would be wrong to push Presley off on the Vice President since it will take very little of the President's time and it can be extremely beneficial for the President to build some rapport with Presley.

In addition, if the President wants to meet with some bright young people outside of the Government, Presley might be a perfect one to start with.

Approve Presley coming in at end of Open Hour _____

Disapprove _____

MEMORANDUM FOR: THE PRESIDENT

SUBJECT: Meeting with Elvis Presley
December 21, 1970
12:30 p.m.

I. PURPOSE

To thank Elvis Presley for his offer to help in trying to stop the drug epidemic in the country, and to ask him to work with us in bringing a more positive attitude to young people throughout the country.

In his letter to you, Elvis Presley offered to help as much as possible with the growing drug problem. He requested the meeting with you this morning when he presented himself to the guard at the Northwest Gate bearing a letter.

II. PARTICIPANTS

Elvis Presley

Bud Krogh (staff)

III. TALKING POINTS

A. We have asked the entertainment industry - both television and radio - to assist us in our drug fight.

B. You are aware that the average American family has 4 radio sets; 98% of the young people between 12 and 17 listen to radio. Between the time a child is born and he leaves high school, it is estimated he watches between 15,000 and 20,000 hours of television. That is more time than he spends in the classroom.

C. The problem is critical: As of December 14, 1970, 1,022 people died this year in New York alone from just narcotic related deaths, 208 of these were teenagers.

D. Two of youth's folk heroes, Jimi Hendrix and Janis Joplin, recently died within a period of two weeks reportedly from drug-related causes. Their deaths are a sharp reminder of how the rock music culture has been linked to the drug sub-culture. If our youth are going to emulate the rock music stars, from now on let these stars affirm their conviction that true and lasting talent is the result of self motivation and discipline and not artificial chemical euphoria.

E. Suggestions for Presley activities:

1. Work with White House Staff

2. Cooperate with and encourage the creation of an hour Television Special in which Presley narrates as stars such as himself sing popular songs and interpret them for parents in order to show drug and other anti-establishment themes in rock music.

3. Encourage fellow artists to develop a new rock musical theme, "Get High on Life."

4. Record an album with the theme "Get High on Life" at the federal narcotic rehabilitation and research facility at Lexington, Kentucky.

5. Be a consultant to the Advertising Council on how to communicate anti-drug messages to youth.

Copy of actual document

Copy of actual document

Front view of Elvis is Alive Museum in the original building

Bill Beeny in Museum

Funeral Room casket reduplicating "Elvis" funeral

Elvis in the service

CHAPTER THREE

In early August 1996, I received a call from the producer of the Rosie O'Donnell Show in New York. They wanted me to fly to New York and appear on her show the day of the Anniversary of Elvis' "Death." I agreed to come and arrangements were made. Within a day or so, I received another interview invitation. This was from Brendon Conway, the producer of the "After Hours Show" on CNBC, also in New York. So I agreed to be on his show after I had done the Rosie O'Donnell Show.

On my way to New York, I stopped off at Washington, D.C. The <u>Real Lisa Marie Presley</u> had flown in from Europe and we were to meet her near Washington D.C. (Many are surprised to learn that Michael Jackson's former wife is not the real Lisa: she is a stand in.) While meeting with Lisa Marie, her husband and two children, I received a phone call. The call was from Rosie O'Donnell's producer stating that my appearance on the show had been cancelled and gave a lame excuse. It is apparent that pressure had been put on Rosie O'Donnell to cancel me. After all, this was August 16th, the day for the candlelight vigil and all the commercial activity at Graceland. The last thing they needed was for me to be on a popular talk show giving facts, irrefutable facts, that proved Elvis was alive.

So, they cancelled me, and, instead, replaced my time slot on the O'Donnell Show with a kid's jumping frogs. I later faxed Rosie that I didn't mind being pre-empted on her show—but by a frog? The CNBC show was still on, however. I received a call at the Mayflower Hotel where we were staying from Brendon Conway. He was a real prince to work with, as well as all the CNBC crew. I learned I would be debating some of the Memphis Mafia on the subject, "Is Elvis alive and did he fake his death?"

I had invited Phil Aitcheson, the founder of The Presley Commission, to be on the show via satellite. Phil, along with the rest of the Commission has done a marvelous job producing "The Presley Report," a very factual detailed report, proving that Elvis faked his death. Phil Aitcheson, along with Gail Brewer-Giorgio, are two of America's leading exponents revealing that Elvis is indeed alive today.

On the other side of the debate, CNBC invited former bodyguard Red West, and Marty Lacker, who is the former boss of the Memphis Mafia. Also in attendance was Larry Geller, who had been Elvis' hair stylist and an FBI agent. Geller was to discuss if it were possible that Elvis could have been put into a witness protection program. Generally, the former aides to Elvis laughed at the idea that Elvis was alive and faked his death. They were not able to answer any of the questions Phil and I put to them. We were happy at the way the debate went, and felt we had done a credible job presenting our facts. They contended there was no donor body.

We came back from New York and only three weeks later, I get a call from CNBC Producer Brendon Conway. He said, "Have you heard the news?"

"What are you talking about?" I said.

He then told me that Marty Lacker (whom we had just debated) and Billy Smith, Elvis' cousin, had just written an article in *People's Magazine* in London. In the article, they confirmed that Elvis did fake his death. He did have a donor body in the casket! Holy-moly, what an about face? Just a mere three weeks before, Marty Lacker was laughing at us on the debate, now he was confirming that what we said about Elvis was right.

The purpose of Brendon Conway's call was to invite me to do a follow-up show on CNBC in light of this new evidence. Marty Lacker, Red and Sonny West all declined to come on the show with us. Phil Aitcheson and I agreed to be on the show. Since these former members of the Memphis Mafia were too red-faced to come back for a second round, the producer got Elvis' half brother to be on the show. This was Rick Stanley, who took the view that Elvis was dead.

Now that some members of the Memphis Mafia had decided to finally tell the truth after nineteen years of silence, the question was "Whose body was donated for the autopsy and burial?"

Phil Aitcheson of the Presley Commission has some of the best evidence on both the autopsy and identity of whose body was in the casket. I obtained permission from him to reprint some of these facts for you. Following is Phil's conclusion as to whom the donor body belonged to.

ELVIS A. PRESLEY—DATE & TIME BRACKETS REVIEW

August 15, 1977

Elvis was preparing for a twelve-day concert tour that was to start in Portland, Maine on August 16, 1977.

Dr. Nichopolous wrote a prescription for "medications" to be filled prior to the tour.

Lisa was still at Graceland on an extended vacation. Elvis spent much of the time playing and riding in golf carts with her.

Elvis called his dentist, Dr. Lester Hoffman to ask him to open the office for an emergency appointment. He had his teeth cleaned and a filling attended to. Elvis, accompanied by his cousin, Billy Smith, his friend Charlie Hodge, and girlfriend-fiancée Ginger Alden left for Dr. Hoffman's office for a 10:30 pm appointment. Elvis was wearing his blue DEA jogging suit.

Notations

Why was Lisa still at Graceland on an extended vacation, when Elvis knew he would be leaving the next day for a concert tour?

How did Elvis find the time to spend with Lisa when he knew he would be going on a twelve-day tour? The most accepted theory is that Elvis took the time with his daughter because he knew that he was leaving and going to be gone for a long time.

Taking into consideration how much Elvis loved Lisa, one would think that he would be busy or his mind somewhat occupied with packing and getting ready for the impending tour. Was this a clue that he wasn't going on a tour at all? It is known that he told at least one individual (Ellen Foster) that he was not intending to go on the tour.

There is some question regarding the individual who would care for Lisa in the event that she would not return to her mother's in California.

Why was Charlie Hodge still at Graceland? It was his responsibility to be the advance man for tours, and for being Elvis' friend. He was supposed to supervise the stage setups, etc. Did Charlie have another assignment? What role was he to play in his friend's leaving? Several books have speculated on this point. See Literary Review.

August 16, 1977

Elvis returned to Graceland from the dentist between 12:30 am and 1:30 am. He was reported to be energetic, optimistic, good-humored, and full of plans for the future.

At 4:00 am, Elvis called Billy Smith and his wife to join him and Ginger on the racquetball court, for an hour's play. Elvis was still wearing the DEA jogging suit. Elvis reportedly whacked himself on the shin, hard enough to leave a knot on his leg, with his racket during the game. This injury was severe enough to leave a mark on his leg. No mark was noted in the alleged autopsy.

At 5:00 am, Elvis sat at the piano in the lounge area of the racquetball building and sang some songs after the game.

At 6:00 pm, Elvis and Ginger went up to his bedroom where he changed into his pajamas (powder blue by most reports), watched T.V. and read.

At 8:00 am, Elvis told Ginger he was going into the bathroom lounge area to read. Note: The bathroom has its own back entrance that leads downstairs.

Between 8:00 and 8:30 am, Elvis calls Dr. Nichopolous at his office, for some sleeping pills, and although he was not there he spoke with the nurse. Nurse Tish Henley instructed her husband to take a couple of pills to be given to Elvis' Aunt who came by, placed in a small envelope, to give to Elvis.

At 9:30 am, Elvis left the bathroom and went downstairs at which time he signed for a special delivery letter from Paul Lichter. See receipt exhibit.

At 10:00 am, Elvis was seen retrieving his newspaper from the porch.

At the very least, three hours transpired before the reported time of the body having been discovered.

Between 2:00 pm, and 2:30 pm, Ginger Alden awakened, making some phone calls, and then remembers Elvis having gone into the bathroom/lounge area earlier to read.

At 2:30 pm, Ginger claims she discovered Elvis' body in the bathroom/lounge area on the floor in front of the commode, where he was purportedly reading, according to police notes. The body was found in a "kneeling" position, with the knees almost touching his chin, resting on the forearms, bent under him, head down, with his face in the carpet. Ginger called down to Al Strada, Elvis' friend/employee who was in the kitchen. Al came upstairs. Then he called downstairs for Joe Esposito, Elvis' friend and staff manager. Dr. Nichopolous was called. Joe, realizing a problem with Elvis, also noticed that

Rigor Mortis had set in, he called the Fire Department, Rescue Unit #6. Joe and others rolled the body over and then he (Joe) started CPR.

At 2:33 pm, Rescue Unit #6 arrived at Graceland. The medics continued CPR, despite the body being Rigor-Mortised and with Lividity.

At 2:48 pm, the body was transported to Baptist Memorial Hospital.

At 2:56 pm, the alleged body of Elvis Presley arrived at BMH, reportedly DOA–(Dead on Arrival).

At 3:00 pm, family and friends were told that Elvis was pronounced dead.

At 3:30 pm, the fans and public were told that Elvis had died.

At approximately 7:00 pm, the body was being prepared for an autopsy.

At approximately 7:30 pm, the initial body inspection was completed. Note: The body inspection is when the Medical Examiner does an external viewing of the body, making notations as to the condition of the body, noting any signs of injury, etc.

At 8:00 pm, Dr. Nichopolous and Dr. Francisco, the Medical Examiner for Shelby County, were interviewed in a press conference.

Notations

For a 10:30 pm appointment, Elvis returns at 12:30-1:30 am. There is a two to three hour dentist appointment. Was there other business for Elvis to complete, other than having teeth cleaned and a filling tended to?

Why would Elvis wear his DEA jogging suit to the dentist? In the normal course of any law enforcement personnel officers, deputies, troopers, or agents don't usually wear uniforms, fatigues, or other official clothing while "off duty."

If a filling was tended to, and Elvis had his teeth cleaned, one would have to presume that something was given to him for the pain. This would more than likely be Novocain and/or some other pain reliever during and after the dental procedure. Why did he have such energy, if he was experiencing pain for the visit to the Dentist?

Why on August 15, did Elvis decide that he needed the dental work done right then? Elvis knew the concert tour was about to begin. Elvis had plenty of time prior to the 15th to tend to the dental work.

A dentist is also usually very careful on doing dental work on a patient with any known heart conditions. The dentist will usually start an antibiotic prior because of the possibility of infection getting into the system during the procedure. How did he get in to see the dentist without prior antibiotic treatment? If the alleged heart condition were charted, antibiotic treatment would generally be required. It may be that there wasn't any heart condition!

It was noted as interesting that the amount of energy Elvis had to play racquetball and sing after a dental appointment, causing some to question the possibility of pain or discomfort affecting him. In much of the research, there are indications that Elvis relaxed by playing racquetball and singing. What had him so uneasy? It is probable that he had some anxieties about the great change that was about to occur in his life.

There are conflicting statements about Elvis' pajamas that he changed into when he was getting ready for bed. The reports signify a color difference. Some reports state that he was wearing powder blue pajamas; some state that the pajamas were blue top and gold/yellow bottoms. Ginger Alden, who was with Elvis when he changed into his pajamas, was up until he went into the bathroom to read, indicates he was wearing powder blue pajamas. All reports from those who observed the body in the bathroom indicate that the pajamas were blue tops and gold bottoms. Could this indicate the person who was wearing powder blue pajamas was not the body in the bathroom?

Elvis left the bathroom /lounge area and went downstairs to sign for a special delivery letter from Paul Lichter. Did Elvis expect the letter to arrive at a particular time? Why did he sign for it himself, when so many others were available to sign for him. (See receipt exhibit, HW-6 & HW-7).

Why was the mail carrier different that day from the usual carrier? The signature on the receipt was not that of the usual carrier. In an interview with a supervisor at the Post Office, the name on the return slip wasn't even recognized as a regular employee. Who was this carrier? And, who did he really work for? The Commission contends that the carrier was someone who was selected to drive the mail vehicle. No one would ever suspect a mail truck coming and going from Graceland at that time of day. The theory being that a body was brought in and Elvis was taken off of the property.

The contents of the letter to Elvis read as a loving "good-bye." Was the letter sent special delivery to insure Elvis received it before he left? This would assure him that he would always be loved and cared about, especially for the person he really is.

At 10:00 am, Elvis was seen picking up his own newspaper off of the porch. His presence was made obvious to others. If he had taken more sleeping pills, why was he still awake? It is probable that he did not take the pills. The call to Dr. Nichopolous may have been to offer a clue to show time factors and/or to let the doctor know he was ready for the plan to be executed.

Between 2:00 pm and 2:30 pm, Ginger stated that she awakened and proceeded to make some phone calls; then, she remembered that Elvis wasn't next to her. How could she not notice if Elvis was in the room with her or not? It is thought that she was more concerned about the phone calls she was making than to check on Elvis first. Did she know about the plan? Was she told to discover a body at a certain time? In the mention of a helicopter being seen at Graceland on the 16th, was this aircraft used to extract the manpower utilized in the removal process, acting as a deterrent?

Between 2:00 and 2:30 pm, a body was found. Many have stated that it did not appear to be Elvis. The body was described as being in fixed Rigor Mortis and with lividity. The positioning of the body was a significant clue, inasmuch as the body could not stay in the fetal position as so described. Muscles tend to relax at the time of death, as the process of Rigor and lividity set in.

A body that is in "fixed Rigor Mortis and lividity" is considered obviously dead. A medic knows you do not do CPR on a body in this state. Anyone working on the body would not have had easy access to the chest area without first breaking the Rigor Mortis, which is not easy and is not really probable. How could anyone get an open airway to give artificial respiration? The jaw is fixed shut, and you can't bend the head back to open the airway. The fixation of Rigor and lividity would have taken eight to twelve hours according to medical advice presented to Commission personnel in recent interviews. It is also stated that when the body was rolled over onto the back a breath was heard. This is normal in almost any incident involving a death. It is the change in the positioning of the body causing expulsion of any air left in the lungs, or the movement of the body might cause an intake of air, sounding like a breath.

There are conflicts as to where the body was actually found. Some reports state:

1. Bathroom in front of the commode
2. Sitting in a chair in the lounge area.

In considering the commode theory, why wouldn't Elvis press the intercom if needed assistance? If he were sitting in the chair, why didn't Elvis pick up the phone and summon for help? In either case, Elvis would realize that something was wrong, or that he was not feeling well. It is human nature to "survive."

In recent interviews with individuals who were on the scene, why did Dr. Nichopolous purportedly order "no drugs" were to be administered for revival purposes? Did he already know it wasn't really Elvis? Was it someone who was already under his care, playing a pre-determined role in an intricate plan?

Why did the medics leave Vernon there? Were they realistically afraid of the stress on Vernon, especially knowing he had a history of heart problems, as well as a recent heart attack. Why would he not go to the hospital with his only son? Was it because he knew that it was not his son? Who really went to the hospital that day? Who was the donor?

In the final analysis, how did the father of Elvis Presley do a radio interview two hours after the death report in a very calm and unemotional state? *Note: see disposition case file.

August 17, 1977

By noon, "the body" was returned to Graceland for private family viewing.

From 3:00 pm to 6:30 pm, the public viewed the body at Graceland.

"The body," reportedly, was dressed in a white suit, blue shirt, and a dark blue tie.

Vernon personally called many fan-club president and personal friends requesting them not to attend the funeral.

Notations

It's reported that the body was changed into a pale blue suit after the viewing. Why change the suit, and how did the family change the clothes on a stiff body?

It is also stated that Elvis' hair was gray around the sideburns, and also gray showing approximately ½ to 1 inch from the scalp. Elvis' own hairdresser is said to have worked all night at the funeral home to dye the hair back to black. It is interesting to note that Elvis was preparing to leave for a twelve day concert tour, and also went to the dentist in the late night/early morning of August 15th and 16th. Elvis was meticulous about his appearance. Would he have gone to the dentist, and been ready to leave at 1:00 am on the 17th for a tour with that much gray hair visible?

Vernon personally called these other people, requesting them to not attend. How could Vernon, a "grieving father" that had just lost his only son be clear-minded enough to make these calls, especially to the personal friends of the family? Why wouldn't Vernon want these people there? Could it be that Vernon was concerned these people would recognize that it was not Elvis? When did Vernon find the time to call all of these people? The only time would've been between 3:00 pm on August 16th after the announcement of the death, and before noon on August 17th when "the body" was brought to Graceland for private family viewing.

It is also interesting to note "the body" was in a white suit. It's reported that Elvis along with Vernon, were seen buying a white suit approximately six to eight weeks prior to August 16th, 1977. Also, on June 14, 1977 Elvis received a phone call from President Carter–a conference call with other White House department heads and advisors. Could that call also have been part of a "plan?" This was also about six to eight weeks prior to August 16th.

In examining the Memphis Press Scimitar, and the Memphis Commercial Appeal from August 17th, 1977, this researcher was unable to locate an obituary for Elvis A. Presley. One would think that there would've been such an item. After reviewing copies of the Scimitar and the Appeal, both from August 17th, an obituary couldn't be located.

August 18th, 1977

Governor of Tennessee, Ray Blanton ordered flags to be flown at half-mast for the funeral procession.

At approximately 2:00 pm, the services started at Graceland. About two hours later, the funeral procession left Graceland heading for Forest Hills Cemetery. The procession had a white Cadillac hearse, followed by sixteen white Cadillac limousines.

There were five official pallbearers, but in many photographs and statements, there were actually ten people carrying the casket.

Notations

Considering the number of people that knew Elvis, especially his father, family members, and other close friends, they would know that Elvis is a spiritual and religious person. Why would services be at Graceland instead of a church?

Through much of the material researched, there are mentions of the sixteen white Cadillacs. Why the "white" Cadillac limousines? A funeral is usually conducted in black. Maybe that is why Vernon was overheard saying he could only get sixteen white limousines, because they usually are black. Could it be that there is a connection or clue to the song, "Mystery Train," and the phrase in the song, "sixteen coaches long, bringing my way back home" as well as the white suit in the '68 Comeback Special?

Also interesting was comments by Elvis' cousin, Gene Smith. During a conversation with a famous author, Gene described the day of the funeral. Gene stated, "The first thing I saw when I went up to the coffin were the hands, and they were not Elvis'. Elvis' hands were big with beat-up calluses on the knuckles, scars, and a crooked finger. All of this from karate, breaking boards and smashing bricks. The hands in the coffin were small, and as smooth as a woman's, smooth as a baby's behind. They were definitely not Elvis'. Plus, the sideburns were glued on; one was sticking straight out at the side. When I noticed this, some man came over and patted it back down like he was sticking it back on. The nose was all wrong—pugged. Elvis had a straight nose. The eyebrows were wrong, the forehead wrong, and hairline wrong. I could even see the hair had been glued on around the forehead–you could see the glue." The question to Gene was, "could it have been a wax dummy?" Gene replied, "Could have been, I thought it was." The next comment was, "Many who viewed the body in the coffin noted what they termed as beads of sweat." Gene answered, "that's true; I saw it too." Gene added, "If it was a wax dummy, then there had to have been an air conditioner in the coffin. I think there might have been. I was one of the ten pallbearers, and that coffin was so heavy I fell to my knees. The coffin was too heavy to have had just a body in it." Gail Giorgio added that "one of Elvis' friends had said the same thing: that he knew it was not Elvis in the coffin, and asked Vernon what was going on, where Elvis was? Vernon told him that Elvis was upstairs…"

Research revealed that there were five official pallbearers, but in many photographs and statements, there are ten. Why ten? Is it because Gene DID disclose the true details? Or, is it because the coffin weighed around nine hundred pounds? A solid copper seamless coffin weighs around three hundred pounds. If a wax dummy were put in the coffin to look like Elvis, then one would suspect that the "hoax" would have to have the approximate weight of Elvis there too, to pull the "hoax" off. Elvis' last known weight was approximately 250 pounds. With the weight of the coffin, and the weight of the wax dummy, that is only 550 pounds. What would leave a 350-pound difference?

While there have been several comments about a wax dummy in the coffin, it was recently brought to the attention of this Commission that a gentleman who worked at a landfill saw a coffin with a wax dummy dumped at the landfill site. If there were a dummy, something would've been used to keep the wax from melting. A cooling system perhaps, or a contained, soundproof freon-circulating system built into the coffin that would run off batteries? The best theory provided that dry ice contained under lining of the coffin along the bottom, with a small built-in soundproof fan to pull off the gases released the dry ice substance. Dry ice would not be detected because there wouldn't be any coolness felt by others passing by the coffin. This would have also explained why no one heard anything as they passed by or stood at the coffin. As long as the units were contained in a sound proof area in the coffin, no sounds would be detected.

Elvis' cousin, Gene Smith stated that the body was "sweating," and that the sideburns along with the hairline seemed to be coming off, and that he could see the glue. Firstly, dead bodies do not sweat. Under the cooling system theory, this commission contends that wax will have condensation. This certainly accounts for the sweating and the hairline problem. The wax, with glue holding hair on, would come up, not due to melting wax, but due to the condensation forming on the wax figure. Considering what Gene Smith had to say, it is the most probable, accurate and truthful statement.

Note: This researcher called a local funeral home regarding the length and width of an average sized coffin. The average is six feet long and 28 to 30 inches wide. A call was also placed to a dry ice company. A block of dry ice that measures eleven inches square would weigh fifty pounds. With these measurements and weight of the dry ice, this would come out to weighing 350 pounds. It is amazing: the missing 350-pound difference mentioned in notation #4 is suddenly accounted for.

One would have to wonder about Vernon's reactions on the day of the funeral. A father that has just lost his only son, so grief stricken he had to leave the mausoleum. However, he was able to conduct business and legal matters that same day. Many court documents show the amount of business that was done that day by Vernon. Was he able to conduct this business because he knew Elvis was upstairs, as Gene stated, that Elvis wasn't truly gone?

The reaction of Colonel Tom Parker leaves many to wonder what he knew. Colonel Parker was reported as being very unemotional. This was a "day of mourning", not a business day. Colonel Parker reportedly shows up wearing a loud short-sleeved Hawaiian shirt and a baseball cap. In further research, has a similar ring to the "hoax". The Colonel was an illegal citizen from Holland; he changed his name, and allowed his family and friends in Holland to believe he was dead. There has been reference to a talk show out of California that had Colonel Parker on. During the interview, the Colonel was asked if Elvis had committed suicide. The Colonel answered, "No sir, he did not! I told him a way out and he took it!" Could this have been a part of a plan, in as much as the Colonel moves to America from Holland, changes his name, and leaves people to believe he had died. Now, Elvis needs to "disappear", what better way then to follow the same type of plan, but for different reasons. The reason being, he needed safety in a life and death situation? **Note**: This Commission found this reasoning to be consistent with the variables that were reviewed in the examination of the pertinent evidence.

It was also noted that Elvis told 2 people that can be found through research that they weren't to worry, when they heard the news of his "death". One person he talked with was his cousin Gene. To show how close Elvis and Gene are, here is some background information on their relationship. Gene Smith was born to Lavalle Smith, Gladys' sister, seven weeks before Elvis was born. Gene grew up with Elvis in Tupelo, Mississippi, where they played together, double dated, and also worked together at Precision Tools, in Memphis. Gene and Elvis were very close, and in fact was a member of the "Memphis Mafia", (Elvis' entourage), until the late 1960's. Gene lived at Graceland, sometimes sleeping in the same room as Elvis, to prevent him from sleepwalking. In Gene's words, "We are closer than brothers". Gene also stated, regarding August 16, 1977, "I saw Elvis a few weeks before August 16th, and he (Elvis) told me, Gene I envy you. You can go anywhere. If you want to stop someplace for a beer, you can. I'm living the most S-O-B 'in life anyone could live"! Gene continued on by saying "Elvis also told me, shortly before the sixteenth, that he would be going away for awhile, but that he would contact me later". Then Gene commented that when he heard Elvis had died, he said he couldn't believe it, felt something was wrong, and then knew something was wrong when he went to the family viewing.

Another person that Elvis told not to worry was Ellen Foster. The conversation took place on August 14, 1977, 2 days before the disappearance. Elvis phoned Ellen, and in the conversation Elvis told Ellen that he wasn't going on the upcoming concert tour, not was he canceling it. Elvis also told Ellen not to worry and not to believe what she reads. He also told her that all of his troubles were ending, and that he felt better than he has for a long time. It was interesting to note that Elvis loved these two people so much that he was concerned about them enough to let them know not to worry.

Sources

Elvis, His Life from A-Z: Worth & Tamerius
The Elvis Files: Was his Death Faked? Gail Brewer-Giorgio
Memphis Press Scimitar: August 17, 1977 issue
Memphis Commercial Appeal: August 17, 1977 issue
Elvis and the Colonel: Velenga and Farren
Elvis, My Brother: Billy Stanley
Elvis Reader: Kevin Quain
The Death of Elvis, What Really Happened? Thompson/Cole
Taber's Cycolpedic Medical Dictionary: Clayton L. Thomas, M.D. M.P.H.
Forensic Pathology: Handbook for the Pathologist and Law Enforcement Personnel: Dr. Fisher M.D. & Dr. Petty M.D.; U.S. Department of Justice
American Medical Association Encyclopedia of Medicine: Dr. Charles B. Clayman, M.D.
If I Can Dream: Larry Geller & Joel Spector
Emergency Care In The Streets: Dr. Nancy Caroline, M.D.
Private, confidential sources in interviews that were held by Commission officials during the course of this investigation, who have requested anonymity concerning their involvement

Drug Area Continuation – III

It is probable that when Colonel Tom Parker made the comment, " I gave Elvis a way out, and he took it", in most probability the body found was Mr. Robert Burl Ross Jr., from Tampa, Florida. There have been comments made to the effect that Mr. Ross had a resemblance to Elvis.

It was also noted that in researched material relative to this matter, there is reference to a "secret" final page of medical report. Under the last section entitled, "Additional Comments: it states, "Clinical studies conducted earlier, indicated that the subject had c.p. (chemically pure) antitrypsin deficiency. This abnormality in the serum was demonstrated on two occasions. The first at Baptist Memorial Hospital, and the second by a sample transmitted to the Mayo Clinic. The Mayo Clinic typed the subject as MS.

In conclusion, it is the expressed opinion of this researcher and the Commission that Elvis A. Presley did not abuse drugs. Elvis may have taken what was needed for any existing medical conditions. The rest of the "drug rumors" are just that–rumors. It is highly possible that these rumors acted as a diversion and/or to use as a tool for "undercover work", keeping in mind that Elvis was and/or is a Federal Agent.

Who is "Ethel Moore, code A77-160"? It is the contention of this Commission that the patient's real identity was Robert Burl Ross Jr., who was found on the floor, autopsied, and the samples studied. This would explain a fictitious name on the file, or that another diversion tool was utilized. The time has come for us to lay the "Drug Abuse" rumors to rest, keeping in mind again that Elvis Presley was/is a Law Enforcement Agent–preventing him from this illegal activity, and in the final analysis, did what he had to do!

DNA Confirms Elvis Lives

Here, in my closing argument I would like to bring several witnesses to testify to the fact that Elvis did not die but faked his death and had a donor body.

The most powerful witness: DNA test. DNA markings are an exact science. They do not lie. The doctor labeling Elvis' tissue specimens was very meticulous. He even had a second doctor check his conclusions to make sure there was no mistake. The LAB TECH laboratory is a highly respected institution. The technicians did not know whom they were testing since it was labeled John Doe #1 and #2, yet the conclusions were very clear. The living tissue of Elvis' biopsy did not match the dead autopsy tissue. They were clearly two different people.

Gene Smith, Elvis' cousin and close confidant said that it was not Elvis in the casket.

Marty Laker and Billy Smith, who for nineteen years contended Elvis was dead, finally in September 1996 admitted in a *People Magazine* article that Elvis faked his death by using a donor body.

Vernon Presley, while at the funeral, admitted to a friend that the body in the casket was not his son, Elvis. Vernon stated, "Elvis is upstairs."

There have been both recorded phone calls and written statements made by Elvis since his supposed death. The phone calls and statements were carefully analyzed by professional analysts; they concluded that the voice and handwriting belonged to Elvis.

Volumes could be written listing hundreds of pieces of evidence, all concluding that Elvis did not die; these books were written by people with credibility. That is not the purpose of this book. The purpose of this book is to relay to the world the fact that Elvis' tissue has been tested and that the clear DNA results state that Elvis' body was not the one taken to the Baptist Memorial Hospital for autopsy. The DNA proves that it is not Elvis' body in the grave at Graceland where millions have walked by in quiet respect and homage. No wonder they did not bury this body next to his mother as Elvis had always requested. Elvis did not want a donor body buried next to his beloved mom. The site next to his mother's grave is still vacant to this day and will only be used when Elvis dies.

Isn't it ironic that after twenty years of hundreds of people looking for the final proof that Elvis did not die, that this proof should come from the grave in the Meditation Garden at Graceland.

The grave at Graceland, which holds the donor body by which millions of ardent fans pass by, cries out today ELVIS IS NOT HERE! HE LIVES! The DNA proves it.

Elvis switched places with a dead man!

TWO former aides of Elvis Presley have come forward with a bizarre claim — they say the King faked his own death with a dying lookalike. They say the superstar desperately wanted to escape the spotlight and start a new life with a wealthy mystery woman known only as Maria. The longtime aides, Marty Lacker and Elvis' cousin Billy Smith, told the British newspaper *The People* an amazing story of Elvis being spirited out of Graceland in the back of a black camper van the day he "died" and simply vanished.

Their hard-to-believe scenario claims that Elvis saw his opportunity for a new life after a chance meeting with a terminally ill man named Scott, who had come to Graceland begging for help for his young family. The King initially agreed to help, say the two aides, but then saw the cancer-stricken man as his way to find a new life. "We were sit-

They insist he really ran off with mystery woman named Maria

ting in Billy's trailer at the back of Graceland one day when Elvis started talking about all the drawbacks and pressures of his life," said Lacker, now a 60-year-old businessman in Memphis.

"He told us, 'I wish I could be someone else living a normal life. I'm tired of all the pressure, tired of all these damn pills and people pulling on me.'" They say Elvis then

A lookalike is in Elvis' grave, claim the aides.

explained his plan, telling them he had met a man with just 18 months to live. On his orders, Scott, who had the same blue eyes and jawline as the singer, had already undergone plastic surgery to become his double. The two men said Elvis told them: "He now looks so much like me I could have sent him down and you wouldn't have known the difference."

In return, they said Elvis promised the man all the money his family would ever want.

Lacker and Smith claim they were ordered to deliver the cash to Scott and were sworn to secrecy.

"We set up a system of cash payments to Scott which I was to see that he got," says Lacker, adding that he and Smith were never told Scott's full identity or address.

Early in 1977, they say, Scott's health began to fail quickly and it became clear he was about to die. Smith says Elvis told him: "We've got some hard thinking to do. If Scott dies out of town, we have to abort the whole damn deal. If we can't make the switch at Graceland, then it's all over."

He and Lacker say Elvis then devised an elaborate plan to sneak the dying man into Graceland, while Elvis and secret love Maria — whom he allegedly met in 1975 — fled in the black camper van. They said by the time the body presumed to be Elvis' was found crumpled on the bathroom floor of his Memphis mansion, the King and his ladylove were hundreds of

claim by ex-aides

ELVIS GOLD DEA BADGE

The King wanted to escape pressure so he faked his death, claim two ex-aides.

The King IS alive!

Trick photography with my wife and "Elvis"

Replica of Elvis tomb at Graceland in Museum

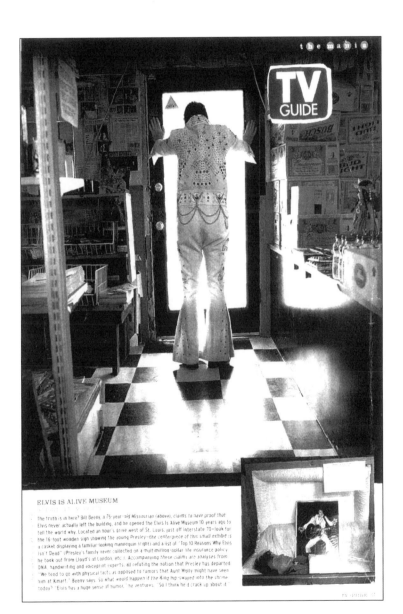

the mania

TV GUIDE

ELVIS IS ALIVE MUSEUM

The truth is in here? Bill Beeny, a 75-year-old Missourian (above), claims to have proof that Elvis never actually left the building, and he opened the Elvis Is Alive Museum 10 years ago to tell the world why. Located an hour's drive west of St. Louis, just off Interstate 70—look for the 16-foot wooden sign showing the young Presley—the centerpiece of this small exhibit is a casket displaying a familiar-looking mannequin (right) and a list of "Top 10 Reasons Why Elvis Isn't Dead" (Presley's family never collected on a multimillion-dollar life insurance policy he took out from Lloyd's of London, etc.). Accompanying these claims are analyses from DNA, handwriting and voiceprint experts, all refuting the notion that Presley has departed. "We tend to go with physical facts, as opposed to rumors that Aunt Molly might have seen him at Kmart," Beeny says. So what would happen if the King swayed into the shrine today? "Elvis has a huge sense of humor," he ventures. "So I think he'd crack up about it

PEOPLE MAGAZINE

7-13-98

upfront

Elvis lives, and Bill Beeny's museum has the proof

MISSOURI

Millions of Elvis devotees flock to Memphis each year to mourn the King at Graceland. But if you're a true believer, you might instead head out on Interstate 70 to the Elvis Is Alive Museum in Wright City, Mo. (pop. 1,250). Don't get all shook up that the one-story museum—with its 16-foot plywood Elvis and 3,500-plus pictures—isn't exactly Las Vegas. And don't expect many genuine Elvis artifacts. But as proprietor Bill Beeny, 71, wearing white, bejeweled bell-bottoms, boasts, "There's no other museum that purports Elvis is alive."

Beeny, no worshiper of the King of Rock 'n' Roll when he opened his '50s-themed cafe a few years after what he terms "Elvis's so-called death," says extensive research convinced him that the FBI had helped Elvis (now 63, but "still very handsome," says Beeny) to disappear. You can watch the hour-long video *The Elvis Files* or buy a $9.95 booklet, *DNA Proves That Elvis Is Alive*. Some visitors say their only disappointment is that the mannequin on display in a satin-lined open coffin doesn't much resemble the King. Replies Beeny: "Neither did the individual in the casket at the funeral." •

"We stay away from it," says Beeny (above), "if it can't be documented."

People Magazine selected the "Elvis is Alive Museum" as the most interesting tourist spot in Missouri

CHAPTER FOUR

In order to simplify the evidence that may well show that Elvis' death was the hoax of the century, I have broken it down into three Categories. They deal with events before his alleged death, the "death" itself, and the strange events after his supposed death. Here we will examine well over a hundred questions, inconsistencies, lies, unexplained facts and testimonies by eye witnesses that may well convince you that Elvis is alive and well today.

Elvis' Pre "Death"

The news traveled like an electric shock around the world on August 16, 1977 reporting that, "The King is Dead." The report stated that Elvis had died sometime between 12:00 pm and 2:00 pm at his home, Graceland. The medical examiner of Shelby County was Dr. Jerry C. Francisco. He stated that Elvis died of hypertensive cardiac vascular disease with arterial scleratic heart disease. A heart attack! Now let us look at some of the strange events leading up to this announcement.

Will Changed

Only nine months before his "death," Elvis changed his elaborate will that included many relatives and friends. The new will only named his father Vernon, and daughter Lisa

Marie. Why? Could it be that he knew he would need the money after his "death?"

Fired Long Time Employees

Sonny and Red West had been with Elvis since high school. They were his bodyguards and had been as close as brothers to him. Yet, they, along with many other long time employees, were terminated in employment shortly before his "death." Others, including his back up singers, were told that they should seek other employment. Was Elvis gently phasing out these workers, knowing that his planned "death" would soon be coming?

Cashed Insurance Policies

In March of 1977, just six months before his "death," Elvis cashed in three paid up insurance policies for a little under two million dollars. This money was legally his. These policies were paid up in full. There was no fraud. There was a fourth not paid up. We will discuss that later as well as one million dollars missing out of his checking account. Why the urgency to raise that large amount of money? Was Elvis putting away a nest egg for the time after his "death?"

Sold Farm

Elvis had a retreat farm just over the Tennessee line that he loved to retreat to with the band and friends. Yet, he sold it and turned it into cash just before his "death". Why?

Elvis' Fan

Elvis had a Fan by the name of Ellen Foster. She looked so much like his mother (now dead) that he gave her a ring. Elvis was to leave on a concert tour the day he "died". Yet, on the 14th of August he called Ms. Foster and told her he would not be leaving on the 16th for the concert tour. She asked him if he was sick, Elvis stated that he was not and that she should not ask any more questions, and that she should not tell anyone of their conversation. The author of "ELVIS...WHERE ARE YOU?" says that Mrs. Foster took a polygraph test about the story and passed it.

Elvis' Weight

At the time of Elvis' "death" those around him state that he weighed about 255. In the past Elvis would crash diet and go down to about 170 before going on a concert tour. Yet the day, August 16, 1977, that he was to leave on concert tour he had no concern about his weight. Could it be that he knew he would not be going this time?

Elvis Liked To Hoax

Those around Elvis verified that Elvis constantly was pulling a hoax on those around him. There were several occasions where he would pretend to faint and be taken to the hospital. Once he set up an elaborate trick on J.D. Sumner and the Stamps Quartet, who were at his home. In the hoax gunmen burst in, shot his bodyguards and a maid. Elvis wanted to see what J.D. Sumner would do. J.D. fell on top of Elvis to protect him. Elvis never forgot this. He showered many expensive gifts on J.D. Could this have been rehearsal for the greatest hoax of all?

Elvis Liked Double Life

Since childhood, Elvis liked playing a double life. As a child, he was fascinated with Captain Marvel, Jr. He imitated his hero. His hero worship was carried over into his adult life with the capes, (worn in concerts) the lighting bolt, which was his logo for TCB (Taking Care of Business) Enterprises. He hero-worshipped The Lone Ranger and other law enforcement officials.

Elvis had a large collection of guns, badges, and authoritative identifications. He was made a real deputy of Shelby County, Tennessee, and would quite often pull over speeders and lecture them.

Elvis wrote President Richard Nixon requesting that he be made a Federal Narcotics Agent at Large. The request was granted. The Justice Department verified that an undercover drug agent traveled with Elvis pretending to be a band member. Elvis loved the secret double life. There were occasions when he wore a ski mask and went on drug raids with narcotics agents.

Once Elvis dressed as a police Lieutenant and attended the funeral of a police officer. Could it be that this life-long desire for a secret double life culminated in the greatest secret double lie of all?

Only Two Jumpsuits

Elvis had hundreds of expensive changes of clothes. Yet, at the weight of 255 only two jumpsuits fit him. Why did Elvis not have new ones made or old ones altered? Could it be he knew he would not need them?

Life In Danger

Elvis' life was constantly in danger. Death threats to himself and his family were received weekly. He had received over three hundred death threats. The FBI files on Elvis contain more than six hundred pages of information about threats against Elvis' life, extortion, kidnap threats, etc. Elvis was under constant, tremendous pressure. He was virtually a prisoner at his home, Graceland. He often stated in later years that it was a miserable life being Elvis Presley. So miserable in fact, that he resorted to heavy use of prescription drugs to make life tolerable. Could it be that his desire for peace of mind, a normal life, freedom of movement, relief from constant death threats and extortion, caused him to carry out the greatest hoax of our lifetime?

Fascination With Death

Those around Elvis did not understand his fascination with death. Elvis would quite often visit the morgue and the coroner's office. He was well acquainted with the Shelby County Medical examiner, Dr. Francisco. He would often spook his friends by taking them to view dead bodies. While in California he took studies in religions of the east. He studied self-hypnosis where he could put himself into a state like death, where the pulse was ever so slight. This could have easily fooled his girl friend, Ginger Alden, who was the first to find him after his supposed death. Did Elvis have a design in all this study and fascination with death?

Savings Accounts Mystery

When an accounting was done of Elvis' financial affairs after his alleged death, it revealed that his three savings accounts had been drained down to near zero. At the same time, his checking account had over one million dollars in it. Later, this million dollars vanished. To this day, there is no explanation as to where it went! Was it that Elvis needed cash now that he would not be performing?

Huge Record Stockpile

At the time of Elvis' alleged death Elvis weighed over 250 pounds. His career certainly was not an all time high. Yet, at this time, a few weeks before his "death", his manager, Col. Tom Parker, placed the largest record order ever; he also stockpiled all other types of Elvis merchandise. In fact, he at that time formed a new merchandising company called Boxcar Enterprises (Inc.) to distribute Elvis merchandise. Why the huge stockpile of records, tee shirts, etc? Did Parker know the coming of "death"? RCA sold over 100 million records. This was a new high. With the "death" of the King, stores could not turn out records, tapes, etc., fast enough to meet the demand! Was this a coincidence or was it planned? The pieces to the puzzle are now beginning to fall in place.

No novocaine

Hours before his "death" Elvis went to the dentist late at night. During the dental work, he was given a novocaine shot. Yet in the so-called autopsy there was no novocaine in his system.

Bad Heart?

The cause of his death, according to the medical examiner was a heart disease. Yet, a few hours before his alleged death, Elvis played racquetball for several hours. Anyone knows that racquetball is a very strenuous sport. Certainly, anyone with bad heart disease would not participate in it.

Lloyds of London Declared Elvis Healthy

It was this company that insured Elvis, yet they gave him a physical exam and declared him in "good health" a short time before August 16th. If he had a prolonged heart disease, how could they have missed it?

Lisa Marie At Mansion

Under the divorce arrangement, Elvis had visiting rights with his daughter Lisa Marie. However, Elvis never left her at the Graceland mansion while he was away on tour. This time, even though he was supposed to have left on the concert tour the day of his "death", Lisa Marie was at Graceland. He had not had her flown back to her mother. Could it be that Elvis wanted her there so that when the news of his "death" came out she would be there to be told the truth?

Nine Hundred Pound Casket

When the news of Elvis "death" went out, almost immediately a 900-pound casket was delivered. Why so heavy? Some who saw the "body" in the casket said it was a wax dummy, and that cool air was coming out of the casket. Friends believed that a cooling unit was in the casket, hence the 900 pounds. It was also questioned how such an unusual casket was ready so fast. Could it be that it had been prepared ahead for this event?

John Burrows – Sivle

Elvis had two aliases he used at times to conceal his identity. One alias was "John Burrows". When he wrote to President Nixon asking to be made a Federal Agent, he told the President that he was registered at the hotel in Washington under the name "John Burrows". He used the name a lot in his undercover drug work for the Justice Department.

He also used the alias "Sivle", which is Elvis spelled backwards. He wore a wrist bracelet with the word "Sivle" on it.

The night after his "death" a man by the name of John Burrows bought a ticket for South America from the Memphis Airport. A man named John Burrows has cropped up several times since Elvis' "death" in connection with the Elvis Presley Enterprises. Likewise, a man named "Sivle" is often seen taking part in the Presley affairs. This seems to be more than a coincidence.

Was Elvis Saying Goodbye?

There were a number of strange and bizarre things, which Elvis did and said just before his "death." Many of his fans feel that he was telling them "good-bye", telling them that his last performances were at hand. Here are some of these strange events.

My Way

Rick Stanley, Elvis' step-brother who wrote in his book "Elvis, We Love You Tender", states that in his last concerts in May and June, that Elvis was very sad, and spoke and sang often about death or leaving. He started closing his concerts with the song "My Way". This starts...."And now the end is near...". One night, conscious of being overweight, he told Rick, "Know what, Rick? I may not look good tonight... but

I'll look good in my coffin." While Elvis weighed 250 pounds, the coroner weighed the supposed corpse of Elvis in at 170 pounds! What happened to the other 80 pounds? Was it someone else in the casket...a wax dummy...or Elvis? Friends and relatives, who viewed the corpse, said it was definitely not Elvis!

Adios!

In Elvis' last concert, instead of his usual closing Elvis closed by saying "Adios" which, of course, means "I'll see you later." Is he doing just that today?

Blue Christmas

Isn't it strange that in his last concerts, which were held in the summer months, Elvis constantly sang the song "Blue Christmas"? This has the phrase. "I'll have a blue Christmas without you." Was Elvis letting his fans know that he would not be around performing at Christmas?

Last Farewell

At his last studio session, one of the last songs he recorded was "Last Farewell." Was this his way of saying goodbye?

Needed Money

In his last televised concert, Elvis was grossly overweight. He normally never wanted his fans to see him over 170 pounds. Yet, at the concert he weighed over 250. Did he do the concert to raise as much money as he could before August 16th?

Wayne Newton

It was just a short time before his "death" that Elvis told Wayne Newton that soon the concert business would be all his. Thus, again saying goodbye?

QUASH. "Elvis Alive Information"

There seems to be a concerted effort by someone, or some group, to nip in the bud the dissemination of any information giving evidence that Elvis is alive. Gail Brewer-Giorgio wrote a book of fiction called "Orion". This fiction told of a Nashville singer who became famous, then tired of it and faked his death in order to live a normal life. Simon and Schuster Publishers paid the author Ms. Giorgio, $60,000.00 advance. They did an about face! They killed the book, took it off the shelves! They tied the book rights up for three years so that no one else could publish it.

Another author, Monty Nicholson, who lived on the other side of the country in California, also wrote a book called "The Presley Arrangement." The book also raised questions about Elvis' *death*. Mr. Nicholson, a veteran police investigator, states that his book was also killed, and removed from the shelves. Yet, neither of these authors at that time knew of one another!

Later they jointly filmed a video named "The Elvis Files". This dealt with the fact that Elvis may be alive and well today. I wanted to order a number of these videos, so I called the distributor in Batavia, Ohio and ordered thirty of the tapes. I was then told that they lost the right to distribute the tape, and there would be no more once the present supply was gone! So once again some force is working to dry up any voice that is saying…"Examine the facts, Elvis may be alive!"

Why So Many Elvis Specials?

There has never been a time when there have been so many nationwide specials on Elvis Presley. As this is being written, in the last four weeks there have been seven nationwide specials on Elvis, either on the networks or on cable. I have noticed that they are ended with a lot of footage dealing heavily on the subject about Elvis' sickness and death. It's like the old adage "Thou doth protest too loudly!" It seems a concerted campaign to squelch any voice which says "Look at the evidence and then you be the judge if Elvis is alive or not.

Elvis' "Death"

There have been a number of deaths in recent years that were that were surrounded by unanswered questions. Some of them are: John Kennedy, Martin Luther King and Marilyn Monroe. But no death in our century has been shrouded in more mystery, questions, concealment, cover up and evasiveness than the death of Elvis. The other deaths dealt with the subject why and how they died, while Elvis' "death" deals with the subjects: Is he dead? And if not: why the hoax?

It is beyond question that many officials, doctors, medical examiners and persons in high office have worked hard at the task of concealing or altering a lot of the facts surrounding the death of Elvis Presley!

Conflicts In Time

No one seems to know the time of day that Elvis "died" in the bathroom of his upstairs bedroom at the Graceland mansion. Ginger Alden says that she last saw him alive at 9:00 am. Some doctors have him dead at 8:00 am. One report states that rigor mortis had already set in by 9:00 am. Yet, it was a full four hours before the paramedics arrived. If rigor mortis had set in at 9:00 am, then why did they try for HOURS to revive him at the hospital? One person who saw his body said he had on blue pajamas, another, the step-brother, Rick Stanley, states he had on a yellow pajama top, a third person there, said the pajamas were black. Did anyone in fact see Elvis' body?

Reason For Death

While the supposed autopsy was still being performed at the Baptist Hospital, the medical examiner went out, met the press, and stated that Elvis died of a heart attack. This was before the autopsy was finished. Later, other doctors stated he had a strong heart and that death came from a combination of prescription drugs. Others reported that he died of bone cancer. What did he die of...? Or, is he dead?

Short Autopsy

A normal non-complicated autopsy report by a medical examiner is usually about 40 to 50 pages long. Elvis' autopsy was only two pages long and left out all the vital information usually listed in an autopsy.

Stomach Contents Disappeared

The most vital part of any autopsy is the contents of the stomach. Yet, the doctors at the Baptist Hospital reported that the stomach contents were flushed down the drain without ever being examined! How very, very strange for experienced doctors to have acted in this way!

Autopsy Ordered By Family

The law states that when a person dies unattended, as was the case of Elvis, that the authorities must order an autopsy. Yet, in this case they did not order one. If they had, it would have been public information. Instead, Vernon, Elvis' father, ordered it and thus it was private. ABC with its 20/20 program sued the Presley Estate trying to get a copy of the autopsy but lost in court. It was kept secret until years later, when it was revealed.

Elvis' Original Death Certificate Lost

A death certificate is usually made out within hours of a death. Elvis' first death certificate was mysteriously lost. Later, his private physician, Dr. Nichopoulos, completed a death certificate.

Two Death Certificates

Later, there was officially two death certificates filed on October 20, a full two months after death.

20/20 Investigation

Geraldo Rivera on ABC's 20/20 stated that the Elvis Presley autopsy and the ensuing reports were the poorest of the century. He stated that no real effort was made to determine the cause of death. (Was there a reason for this cover up?) Here are some things that 20/20 report brought out.

No Police Investigation

It was nine in the evening, long before the autopsy was completed that the police department closed out their investigation. His body was taken to a funeral home owned by a friend of the family. Elvis was close to the Memphis police department

No Drugs Found At Graceland

The medical examiner stated that the house at Graceland was searched for drugs but none were found, and no search was made of the Nurses' trailer.

Stomach Contents Destroyed

The stomach contents were destroyed without ever having been analyzed.

There Never Was A Coroner's Inquest
D.A. Not Notified

The Shelby County District Attorney was never notified as to whether there was a violation of criminal law.

Drugs – Where?

No attempts were made, even after the toxicology reports, to find where Elvis got all his prescription drugs.

Documents – Pictures Disappear

All of the photographs taken at the death scene, all notes of the Medical Examiner's investigation, all of the toxicology reports allegedly prepared by the Medical Examiner, are missing from the official file.

Cover Up?

Officials of the County Government believe there has been a cover up.

Elvis Filled Out His Death Certificate?

One handwriting expert, Paul Weist, compared known writing of Elvis with the handwriting on his death certificate, and came to the conclusion, after exhaustive investigation and thorough study, that the handwriting was the same. Elvis had filled out his own death certificate after his "death" according to Mr. Weist.

Fans Believe Him Alive

Is it any wonder that a recent survey of people who had been given all the facts, revealed, that 84% believed that Elvis is alive today. There had been too many lies, cover up, deceit by doctors, officials and others. You can't fool all the people all the time!

Cousin...." Not Elvis.."

Among the many spectators who viewed the body, which was supposed to be Elvis, was Gene Smith, Elvis' cousin. Mr. Smith was very close to Elvis. He grew up with Elvis. He worked for him. He was around him at Graceland on a day-to-day basis. If anyone knew Elvis, it was Gene Smith.

Mr. Smith did a video documentary in which he categorically denies that the body in the casket was that of Elvis. He noted the following differences:

The body in the casket did not look like Elvis. The body had a "pug nose". Elvis had a more pronounced nose.

Elvis was into Karate and broke bricks with his hands. Therefore, they were rough, with enlarged knuckles. The body had smooth hands.

One side of the face had a side-burn sticking out an inch from the head; it had come unglued.

Mr. Smith noticed glue along the hairline. It appeared to him that a hairpiece had been glued on.

Mr. Gene Smith (Elvis' first cousin) concluded that whoever or whatever was in the casket, one thing for certain it was NOT Elvis!

Dad – Not Elvis

When a songwriter and friend of Elvis (he wanted his name withheld) told Vernon (Elvis' Dad) that the body was not that of Elvis, Vernon stated, "Yes I know, we have his body upstairs."

Daughter Unconcerned

Priscilla Presley, Elvis' divorced wife states that she flew from California to Memphis immediately upon hearing of his death. She stated when she got to Graceland, (sometime after midnight) Lisa Marie, their daughter, was out riding the golf cart around on the grounds. How strange that if Elvis were truly dead, his nine year old daughter would not be in sorrow, certainly not out playing with a golf cart. Many feel that Elvis had her at Graceland at the time the "death" news broke so she could be told the truth.

Colonel Tom in Charge

Elvis' long time manager Col. Tom Parker was in charge at the funeral. He hired a comedian, Jackie Kahane, to deliver the eulogy. How strange! Next, he hired an outside minister–not Elvis'–to give an address. Third, he hired a second outside TV evangelist Rex Humbard, (Elvis had only met him once briefly) to give a second address. Many around the Colonel said he was laughing, joking and on the phone putting together merchandising packages as though Elvis had never died.

Colonel Busy

The Colonel hurriedly left Memphis for New York to put together the largest Elvis Presley marketing deal yet. It involved millions of records, tons of merchandise and millions of dollars. Elvis loomed much larger in "death" than in life. Yet, two years later, after Vernon's death, a probate court stripped Col. Tom Parker of all his right to merchandise Elvis Presley. The court stated that his cut was excessive.

Name Misspelled on Gravestone

Vernon Presley, Elvis' dad selected the gravestone. No one can explain why, but he misspelled Elvis' name on the gravestone. Elvis' name was ELVIS ARON PRESLEY. The gravestone (which I recently saw at Graceland) is spelled Elvis AARON PRESLEY. Used two A's in the middle name. No one to this day knows why, except it was Vernon's way of saying "Elvis is not in the grave."

Mother Moved Next to Elvis

Elvis loved his mother very much. While a child and growing up she had sacrificed everything for him. He always wanted to be buried next to her. Therefore, when he died and was placed in a white marble crypt, her body was disinterred and placed in a crypt next to his. Then Vernon applied for a zoning change so that the bodies could be interred at Graceland. Vernon was afraid someone would break into Elvis' casket. It is strange that when the bodies were moved to Graceland that Vernon did not honor Elvis' request to be put next to his mother. Instead, if you go to Graceland today, you will see Elvis' grave is between Vernon and his aunt. The mother's grave is on the other side of Vernon's. Again raising the question, is Elvis' body really in the grave?

Grave Break-In

Vernon's fears came true. Only two weeks after Elvis' "death" three men tried to break into his crypt. They did not want the body, they stated, they just wanted to prove that Elvis was not in the casket. The matter was hushed up; Vernon dropped the charges. A lawyer stated that had they been successful and broke into the crypt for all to see what was inside, "all hell would have broken loose in Memphis."

Bodies Moved Again

Now there was talk and pressure from fans to have Elvis' body exhumed and checked. This talk unnerved Vernon. They rushed the zoning change through, and on October 2, 1977, about six weeks after his death, Elvis and his mother's bodies were supposedly moved to Graceland. Elvis' "body" was put under tons of granite. There would never be an exhuming of the body now. The seamless coffin would never be opened now. Was the truth about Elvis sealed in that coffin?

No Bill for Moving Elvis' Body

A Memphis newspaper ran the following article: "A $23,789.73 claim–filed against the estate of Elvis Presley." They went on to say, "it was for the moving of the body of Gladys Presley..." They let the cat out of the bag. No charge for moving Elvis, only Gladys. Did they move Elvis' body free? Not hardly. You draw your own conclusions.

Money Rolls in for "Dead Elvis"

The Colonel's marketing plan worked. The week after Elvis' death twenty million records sold. This soon soared to over 100 million records. The presses couldn't keep up with the demand. The Kind was making more money in "death" than in life. He generates over one-half billion dollars annually in sales.

Fan Club President asked not to attend Funeral

Many of the fan club officers were disturbed when Vernon asked them not to attend the funeral, but to wait later to come to Graceland. It was like he did not want those who knew him best to see him in the casket. Remember, long time employees had already been dismissed. The regular minister did not conduct the funeral. What was the reason for keeping so many people who knew him best away from the funeral?

La Costa..."Not Elvis"
In the Elvis Special Program, they quoted country singer La Costa (Tonya Tucker's sister): "We went right up to the casket and stood there, and God, I couldn't believe it. He looked like a piece of plastic lying there. It didn't look like him at all...he looked more like a dummy than a real person. You know a lot of people think it was a dummy. They don't think he's dead!"

Not Recognize Me
Elvis often studied books on spiritualism as well as the Bible. In one of the books on spiritualism he underscored the following: "Should I return you would not recognize me."

Wearing Chai
Shortly before his "death" Elvis, who believed strongly in symbolism started wearing a "Chai." This ornament of spiritualism means "new life." Was he telling us something?

Million Dollars Missing
Remember, a short time before Elvis' "death" he started raising cash. He cashed in three paid up life insurance policies, sold a retreat farm he loved, did a televised concert to make money even though he was eighty pounds overweight, liquidated all his savings accounts. However, there was a checking account with over one million dollars in it. This money disappeared shortly after his "death." No one to this day knows what happened to it.

No one has claimed his Death Insurance

Elvis had a large term death policy with Lloyds of London. They had given him a physical a short time before his "death," and he was pronounced to be in good health. Why does this contradict the autopsy report stating he had prolonged heart disease?

The big question is: Why to this day the family has not collected on the large death policy? If they collected and he was not dead, this would be insurance fraud, a felony. Is this why they won't collect the insurance money? You be the judge.

Many Items Missing

The inventory made immediately after his death was eighty-four pages long. Yet, there were hundreds of items missing. Missing was most all his jewelry. Elvis had a vast amount of rings, bracelets, necklaces, pendants, etc. Yet, the inventory listed only six pieces of jewelry. His diaries were missing. All the pictures of his mother, which he cherished, were missing. Also missing were family pictures and hundreds of personal items. Two air planes were missing and one million dollars in cash. Who quietly packed and took all this? You be the judge.

Wedding being performed on Elvis stage in front of the Museum

Bill Beeny at his Elvis gift shop located in the Union Station, St. Louis

Elvis impersonators from all over the world visit the Museum

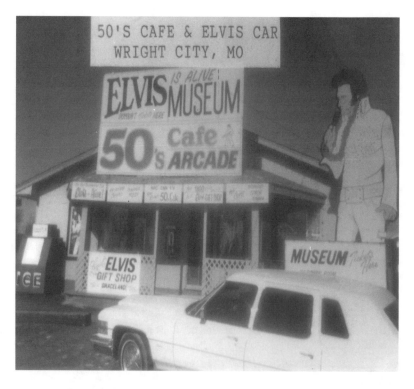

50's Cafe & Elvis Car

CHAPTER FIVE

Post Death

Now we move into the third and final phase of the mysterious scenario. We will sift through the mirage of events, which have taken place since the "death" of Elvis. Here we will see many verified sightings of Elvis, verified handwritings by him since his "death," the roll of the FBI reports. We will examine audiotapes of Elvis' voice since his "death," certified by experts as being that of Elvis. Audio analysis proved it to be his voice. What more proof do we need?

Family Hides Autopsy

ABC's 20/20 wanted a copy of Elvis' autopsy report from the Baptist Hospital. The Presley estate refused to divulge it. The medical examiner would not surrender it. ABC sued and went to court; a judge ruled the family did not have to let the world see what was in the autopsy report. What were they hiding? Why all the secrecy?

Dr. Nick Cover-up

Elvis' family doctor whom he called Dr. Nick also did a cover up. Dr. Nick had borrowed $200,000 from Elvis in 1975. He was in serious financial trouble–over 5.5 million dollars—due to a professional building he owned, which was only one third occupied. Two years later, with his financial affairs getting worse, he borrowed another $55,000 from Elvis. He traveled with Elvis. He supplied Elvis with pain killing drugs. Elvis had a lower bowel problem, which kept him in constant pain. He took large amounts of codeine, which was supplied at will by Dr. Nick.

Fake Death Certificate

Dr. Nick made out a death certificate for Elvis shortly after his "death." This was totally illegal. Only a county medical examiner could do this. Dr. Nick supplied Elvis with thousands of pain pills, sleeping pills, uppers and downers in a short span of a few months. Later the State Medical Board suspended his license to practice for a period of time because of the over dosage of prescription drugs which he prescribed for Elvis. It was excessive.

Taking into account the fact that he was heavily indebted to Elvis, that he loved him like a son, rather than see him kill himself with drugs trying to keep up his grueling schedule, Dr. Nick would have assisted Elvis in any plan or hoax that would have brought him peace of mind and happiness.

Remember, Elvis at this point was constantly, publicly saying, "I hate this life of being Elvis Presley...I am a prisoner in my own home." Along with that, consider the weekly death threats against him and his family. Added to this were his mysterious involvements with the justice department as a drug agent at large and the fact that an undercover federal drug agent was traveling with him posing as a band member. Is it any wonder that he had to have some relief and perhaps the only way out of this was to hoax his death? Many, many people have pretended to die for many reasons and have gotten by with it. Why not Elvis also?

KCOP Television, Los Angeles – 10:00pm News
January 8, 1986

Tim Malloy, co-anchor with Wendy Rutledge. The title of the news segment: LONG LIVE THE KING. The transcript begins with Tim Malloy, speaking:

"Well, now here's a story about Elvis that probably belongs in the twilight zone or more appropriately the night gallery, because it is about a picture, a picture taken after the king's death, one that has made people wonder if Elvis has left this world, or at all? Bob Walsh has more on this mysterious story."

(Bob Walsh's voice)

"Mike Joseph took his family to Graceland for a vacation on January 1st of 1978, more than four months after the death of Elvis Presley–perhaps we should say 'reported death!' At the time, the grounds of Graceland were the only part of the estate open to the public, but Joseph took some snapshots and put them away for safe-keeping.

Four years later while reading about Presley, Joseph took out his mementos of the Graceland visit, and he noticed something unusual in a shot of the bathhouse behind the mansion. It was a shadow in the lower half of the door. Joseph says he had the pictures enlarged and the results were nothing short of startling. Someone or something bearing a remarkable resemblance to Elvis Presley was indeed sitting behind the door. *Playboy* Magazine bought the temporary rights to the pictures for an undisclosed amount of money but never published them. Joseph says *Playboy* and other publications who bid on the pictures weren't sure of just exactly how to handle the story."

(Mike Joseph now speaks)

"They thought it was the most amazing photograph they've ever seen. Everybody, ah, they didn't know what to think–how to present it–I just told them, just present it as a photograph that was taken four months after he died."

(Back to Bob Walsh)

"The picture in question is part of a set. All the negatives are intact, and a spokesman for *Playboy* confirms that the pictures were not doctored. The sequence of pictures was indeed taken after Presley's death. Joseph says he's not trying to convince anyone that Elvis still lives or that the snapshot is an image of some supernatural phenomenon but there is something there. How it got there and what it is will no doubt remain as much a mystery as the entire Presley mystique."

Elvis Maid Thinks He's Alive

A maid named Daisy worked for Elvis for nine years, and had the following to say in an interview:

"I find it hard to believe that he died. There are just too many things that don't seem right. I wish they would dig up that casket and see what is in it. He used to tell me that he was fed up with everything. 'Daisy,' he said, 'I wish I could go off and live by myself and not tell anybody where I am. Maybe on a island somewhere far away!'" (D.M. Williams in an interview with the Globe.) People of all walks of life, from celebrities to the common man don't believe Elvis is dead. They ask, "Where is he?"

Correspondence from Treasury Department

Correspondence received from the Department of the Treasury, and Bureau of Alcohol, Tobacco and Firearms.

"During the period of 1974 through 1976, Mr. Presley provided one of our undercover (narcotics) agents, who was a musician, a job cover. Mr. Presley confirmed to anyone inquiring that the agent/musician was a member of one of his traveling bands. Although Mr. Presley was not actively involved in any of the investigations, his assistance in this regard made it possible for our agent to develop a number of quality investigations."

While I was recently visiting Graceland I noticed in the Trophy Room that Elvis had been presented a Certificate of Appreciation by the Bureau of Alcohol, Tobacco and Firearms by the Regional Director of BATF in 1976.

Many feel that Elvis worked with the government in convicting drug dealers much more than the public knows. He wrote to President Nixon that he would help in any way he could in the war against drugs. This might explain the many and constant threats upon his life. There is also the possibility that he may well be in the government witness protection program. Witnesses who have worked against criminals and testified against them have gone into this program. No witnesses who having stayed in this government program have ever been found or harmed. Could Elvis be there?

Merle Haggard

Country singer Merle Haggard categorically states that he thinks Elvis is alive and well.

Elvis' Stepmother Called

Dee Presley, Elvis' stepmother reported that in 1978, that she thinks Elvis phoned her. It sounded like him and he discussed things that only the two of them knew about.

John Burrows Calls Burt Reynolds

Burt Reynolds, a friend of Elvis, was a guest on a talk show. A caller identified himself as John Burrows (this is an alias Elvis often used). Reynolds was so flabbergasted that they had to go to a commercial.

Sighted in Kalamazoo, Michigan

There have been too many sightings of not only Elvis, but of Lisa Marie as well in Kalamazoo, Michigan, to list here. Suffice to say Kalamazoo is near the home of one of Elvis' friends, former heavyweight boxing champion Mohammad Ali.

Elvis with Ali

Some years after the death of Elvis, a Cincinnati paper printed a picture of Mohammad Ali leaving the hospital. With him were Jesse Jackson and an unidentified black man. Then there was a fourth man who was a dead-ringer for Elvis. When this came out, a reporter (who looked nothing like Elvis) stated that it was he not Elvis.

However, the picture was sent to a facial analysis expert. After comparing the picture to one of Elvis, the expert concluded that the person in the photo was indeed Elvis and not the reporter. So, the evidence continues to pile up that Elvis is alive and well today.

KEEN Radio

A disc-jockey who was with KEEN Radio in San Jose, CA received a strange telephone call from a man identifying himself as "Sivle" (This is also an alias Elvis used. It is Elvis spelled backwards.)

Ray Pennington

This man is a songwriter. He wrote "Ramblin Man." He has worked for Elvis. He stated, "I think Elvis is alive... Nothing adds up."

Fan Sees Elvis in Atlanta

He told Elvis, "I can't believe it's you!" He said Elvis adjusted his glasses and smiled sheepishly and said, "Man you ain't seen me, okay?"

Mystery Tape

There is a mystery tape that was given to Gail Brewer Giorgio, author of the book "ORION." Allegedly the voice of Elvis, it was given to her by an in-law of Elvis. She was told to have a voice print expert check it and they would find that it was Elvis. It is believed the voice was recorded in about 1981. The tape was about one hour long.

Voice print expert L.H. Williams of Houston, Texas compared the mystery tape voice with that of a known voice tape of Elvis. After exhaustive study, he came to the clear conclusion that the voice was the same. It was the voice of Elvis.

In the tape, he talked of traveling around the world, of going back to Germany, where he was in the service. He spoke of wearing a disguise, the fear of being discovered, of running into people who recognized him. This appears to be one more piece to the puzzle that Elvis is alive and well.

The Elvis Special

In one newsletter from the fan club paper called "The Elvis Special," they printed the following:

"We have received startling news from four different people from Louisville, Kentucky. A TV news program ran a story that a plane has seen found registered to Elvis and, apparently, being lived in by an unknown person. The plane is large, with all the comforts of home and even has a swimming pool area. People are asking if Elvis is living in it."

I have been in the LISA MARIE, a Convair 880 that Elvis owned and had converted to all the comforts of home. This plane is at the Graceland Complex. Elvis spent a lot of time on planes and could easily live on one for a period of time.

Masked Elvis

Shortly after the "death" of Elvis, a masked Elvis imitator appeared from out of the blue. His name was Jimmy Ellis. He obviously had a lot of money behind him. He recorded albums on the Sun label. This was the recording company Elvis originally started out with.

He took the name "Orion," obviously from the book ORION. He held large concerts. Orion was very talented and really did not need to imitate anyone. Then rumors began to circulate that there were TWO masked Orions. Some noted that one would sing one part of a concert and the second one the other part. On some occasions, they would be booked in different cities on the same night.

Some who know Elvis well sat on the front row and stated that there was no question but that one of the Orions was Elvis! Was it another shrewd way for Elvis to continue to perform? Suddenly Orion disappeared as quickly as he had appeared. He has not been heard of since.

Monty Nicholson Pictures

Mr. Nicholson, a long time law enforcement investigator, relates that a fellow officer stated that he had worked for Elvis. Also that he had a picture of Elvis getting on a government helicopter after his alleged death. He showed these pictures to Mr. Nicholson. Later, when Mr. Nicholson was writing his book "THE PRESLEY ARRANGEMENT" he contacted this officer to see about borrowing the photos. He was surprised when the man said he knew nothing about the pictures and denied working for Elvis. Mr. Nicholson set a meeting with this officer, (who had now left the force) then he discovered the former officer had given him an address of an empty house, and a disconnected phone number.

Elvis Letter

In a 1979 issue of The Elvis Special, Maria Columbus and Jeannie Tessum reported receiving a message from a friend who simply signed it J.B. (John Burrows? Elvis alias) It read as follows:

Before I left, my thoughts were of all of you. I wanted to leave behind beautiful memories for all of you to share. You see, I knew you loved me and you would grieve deeply for me. I wanted you to remember me with smiles and love of a favorite song, concert or dreams, goals and ideas with people I love.

Now when I should be at peace and you should be going onward and growing, I feel so much hate, envy and jealously...instead of leaving beautiful thoughts behind me. I find only rubbish down as guidelines from friends wanting the public to know the truth of the legend known as Elvis Presley.

Just what is truth my friends?

Is truth calculated as money?

Is truth known in friendship?

Is truth known in love?

Is truth known in caring?

Just what is it? I need to know! I want you to know I gave all of these in loving moments in time. I shared myself and found out that I shared it with Judas–<u>friends</u> that would turn against me after death who did not have the <u>courage</u> to face me in life. This is a reason for dying!

Thank you Dee, Rick, David, Red, Sonny, David, Lamar, and all the others to follow. Thank you for letting the TRUTH out since I am not allowed to contribute to the great array of intelligent blood-letting. But, may I ask one question? If this is the truth, what must your lies be??

I've always been hungry for love and affection. I thought <u>my</u> friends could help, but I found out that <u>my friends</u> and certain (ex) relatives only wanted two things…money and fame. Well folks, you got it.

I wish you many, many years of love and enjoyment from life. But I have to say that you will have these <u>truths</u> on your conscience. Perhaps in a latter life, you can work off the Karma for putting the fans, who love me, through Hell. I'll pay for any Karma I have performed. You are lucky—you have time. I send love and healing to all the people that love me.
Thank you for believing in me.

J.B.

Witness Program

Why would Elvis want to hoax his death? Apart from being miserable, of having no privacy, a prisoner in Graceland, a grueling schedule there were other problems.

There are over 600 pages in the FBI files dealing with the death threats on Elvis' life and the lives of his family, over 300 death threats. Many extortion plots and threats of kidnapping! Elvis was an undercover narcotics agent for the Feds. He had an undercover narcotics federal narcotics agent posing as a member of his band. It could very well be that his life was in more imminent danger than anyone realized. He could very well have been taken into the federal witness protection program. Many have gone into that program never to be heard of again. This would serve a dual purpose, giving him protection from the death threats and at the same time, the privacy which he had long desired. You be the judge!

Priscilla–Another Time

Apparently, Elvis and Priscilla were very much in love, even after divorce. Priscilla kept the Presley name; she never remarried, even after he "died." Priscilla stated as they were separating, "they talked about being together at another time and another place."

Elvis In Kalamazoo

Numerous people have reported seeing Elvis, Priscilla and Lisa in Kalamazoo, Michigan. Many of these are not Elvis fans. There is a hotel in a small Michigan town that has a private, secluded suite occupied by a man known as John Burrows (Elvis alias). This man does a YMCA karate workout there regularly. A disk jockey named Doc Vorb in Louisville, Kentucky stated openly that he believes Elvis is alive. He has evidence that Elvis owns a small hotel in Michigan.

Ali Confirmed Elvis Alive

According to a recent video documentary, Mohammad Ali confirmed that Elvis visited him in the hospital in November 1989. Ali lives just outside of Kalamazoo, Mich. He and Elvis had been close friends for years.

Billy Stanley Verified

A picture taken in 1989 of Ali leaving the hospital with a man who looked like Elvis was verified by Billy Stanley (Elvis' step-brother) to be Elvis. A study done by a facial analysis expert confirmed that it was Elvis.

Here South Korea TV flew a crew to film Museum

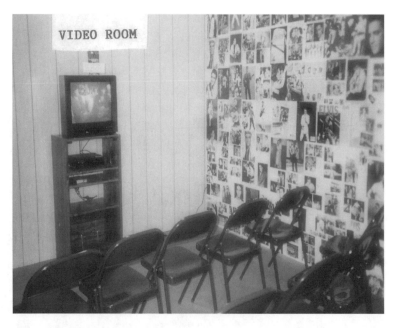

On the TV monitor in the Museum, we play movie documentary of "Elvis is Alive" with Bill Bixby

Museum is located in Wright City, Missouri, which is fifty miles west of St. Louis on I-70 Highway

LEGEND IN HIS TIME!

ELVIS PRESLEY! The name Elvis, according to a Gallop Poll, is the best-known single name in the world .

- During his lifetime, up to his "death" he generated over 40 billion dollars of business by his recording, movies, concerts, sales merchandise, etc.
- He made millions of dollars income and gave away hundreds of thousands of dollars.
- He starred in 33 movies.
- He sold over 1 billion records.
- He had 60 single and 35 album platinum records.
- He had 110 gold records with sales exceeding 120 million.
- He made more money after his "death" than he did before.
- His home in Memphis is the second most visited home in the U.S., the White House being first.
- Last year his home, Graceland, took in over 12 million dollars.
- 15 years after his "death" there are dozens of T.V. specials annually, hundreds of books, his records, tapes, CD's and videos are still all hot sellers.

- What was the magic about the poor boy born in Tupelo, Mississippi who rose to the very top of the celebrity world?
- He was made a Federal Narcotics Agent-at-Large by President Nixon.
- He was voted the Young Man of the Year by the National Jr.
- Money had little meaning to Elvis. Volumes could be written about the hundreds of thousands of dollars he gave away in the form of cash, automobiles, jewelry, etc.

Index